STILL AMIDST THE STORM

Peace! Be still!

Corr Gallagher

STILL AMIDST THE STORM

A Family Man's Search for Peace in an Anxious World

Conor Gallagher

TAN Books
Charlotte, North Carolina

Cover design by Caroline K. Green

ISBN: 978-1-5051-1266-5

Published in the United States by
TAN Books
PO Box 410487
Charlotte, NC 28241
www.TANBooks.com

Printed in the United States of America

ACCLAIM FOR
Still Amidst the Storm

"Who among us can say they don't spend a considerable amount of time struggling with anxiety and worry? In his new book, *Still Amidst the Storm*, Conor Gallaher helps us reflect on how habits of worry and anxiety are easy to fall into. But therein lies an opportunity to grow closer to God, one another, and the peace we all seek.

"His insights from everyday life experiences are wonderful, relatable to our own, and his reflections point us to innumerable ways we can enrich our lives through everyday occurrences. I found it hard to put the book down and found myself reflecting often on his conclusions and suggested roadmap to a better, more fulfilling, and peaceful life in a very busy and noisy world.

"An exceptional read penned by an exceptional young man."

Alan Napleton, president of the
Catholic Marketing Network

"In this book, Conor has given a great gift to every spouse and parent who is looking for God in the midst of married and family life. It is an oasis of wisdom and refreshment for the weary and tired. It's a gift!"

Fr. Jeffrey Kirby, best-selling author
and Crux contributor

"For Conor Gallagher, everyday moments are parables that can enlighten and transform us. He shows us how to find deep within the present moment a rich spiritual significance if we're willing to cultivate silence and stillness. In doing so, of course, he echoes the wisdom of another Teacher who once taught through parables, whose words calmed the sea and gave birth to *Still Amidst the Storm*."

Paul Thigpen, best-selling author of
Manual for Spiritual Warfare

"Carpe momentum! This little book chronicles a Catholic father's quest for peace and presence in a world that would tear us from what we love most. Written with humility and humor, it is perfect for a men's or women's retreat, or as a retreat in itself. Wonderful!"

Suzanne Cona, Charlotte, NC

"As I began to read Conor Gallagher's latest, I knew from past experience and from our friendship, that this book would be woven from two main elements—reality and creativity; or, we might say, the practicality of this world and the hilarity and inspiration which lift us heavenward! Quickly, I found myself wondering if Conor hadn't been hiding somewhere in the Garden of Eden, watching the whole enactment of original sin while learning the deeper lessons about our human nature! Anyone who reads this delightful stream-of-consciousness writing, while also being open to the sometimes gut-wrenching 'Oh my! That scalawag is me!' will find it to be an examination of conscience laced with nuggets of pure delight! I know I did and I hope many, many people will as well! Only one request: *in your next book, Conor, could you please give an uplifting story about us Religious Sisters*?! *Okay, you are forgiven*—and yes, I will be sharing this book with countless of my friends as all of us have something vital, spiritually speaking, in common: original sin and the desire for holiness! To reach that holiness, self-knowledge is essential and Conor has nailed us all (and himself too) spot on!"

Sister Joseph Andrew Bogdanowicz, OP,
Dominican Sisters of Mary, Mother
of the Eucharist, Ann Arbor, MI

"This little gem of a book is not worth the price that is being charged for it because it is priceless. It contains whispered wisdom in a world of noise; a sacred stillness in the midst of life's stampede. It teaches us to take time so that we don't waste it. Indeed it shows us that the gift of life is gained in time taken and is lost in time wasted. It shows us that our lives are, in Hopkins' timeless words, "soft sift in an hour glass". For this reason, the time taken to read this book will save so much time which might otherwise have been wasted. It is, therefore, time well spent."

Joseph Pearce, best-selling author

"With his newest book, Conor draws the reader on with his delightful mix of classical, yet comic perspectives, taking on the real day-to-day challenges of married and family life and inserting them into the beauty of God's plan for our salvation and sanctification. An enjoyable and inspiring read!"

Mother Dolores Marie, PCPA, Our Lady of the Angels Monastery

To the man who even the wind and sea obey

Contents

PART 3: STILLNESS

CONCLUSION

Preface[1]

This book was an accident.

My wife and I married young, and I've been busy ever since. We have twelve kids (yes, all biological and one wife), I run a business, sit on too many committees and boards, coach little league, and eat too much junk food. I also sporadically work out too hard to the point of injury. I hate feeling "plugged-in" all day and despise (with sinful wrath) sitting in traffic. Sometimes I feel the world is running me ragged and that I am only good at a lot of things but not great at anything. I have been too busy being busy.

Know the feeling?

I am very concerned that my children are too modern. We homeschool and raise them in a traditional environment, but I still find my three-year-old hiding with an iPad, playing Internet games, and my heart sinks.

---

[1] There is a difference between a preface and an introduction. A preface is about the book as a book: how and why it came into being. An introduction is about the content of the book.

My pressing question: Am I failing? Have I succumbed to the trappings of the modern world?

The haunting answer: Too early to tell.

Nonetheless, I have become obsessed with the question "how does my family find peace in an anxious world?" I feel pressure to find an answer (quickly) because my kids keep getting older, despite my direct orders to stay young and innocent forever.

Even with twelve kids, I will eventually run out of opportunities to get this stuff right. Lord, have mercy on me.

The original chapters of this book were half-baked journal entries I intend to give to my children. I want them to know my thoughts on important subjects. And the more I focused on the subjects contained therein, the more I saw that everyone—*everyone*—is battling the same issues in the modern world.

There is an epidemic of anxiety. Lord, have mercy on us all.

I did not sit down to write a book. The truest critique of this book is that it isn't much of a book. It lacks cohesiveness. It does not logically unfold like a treatise. It certainly lacks research. What it does have, however, is the heartfelt reflection of a Christian husband and father who is trying to get it right. The book is a series of reflections on real life experiences, experiences that most people have every day.

If this book is worthy of your time, it's not because I am

unique but because I am common. I am like any other husband, father, employee, or employer.

I am a mere family man seeking stillness amidst the storm.

Conor Gallagher
Easter Sunday 2018

INTRODUCTION

FEELING TORN APART

Or

How the Present Moment, Silence, and Stillness Will Put You Back Together

"As for you, son of man, groan! with shattered loins and bitter grief, groan in their sight." Ezekiel 21:11 (NABRE)

Saint Hippolytus of Rome (AD 170–235) had his feet and hands tied to horses and was ripped apart. Many saints have been quartered. Horses were used in ancient times. Machines were used in the Middle Ages and perfected in England during the Reformation.

We say things like, "I feel torn," or, "The death of his wife tore him apart." What a vicious metaphor! I hesitate to use it out of respect for St. Hippolytus and all those

Jesuits on Queen Elizabeth's rack. I don't go around saying, "I feel crucified," or, "I feel skinned alive." Nonetheless, I will use *torn* to describe something. Perhaps I should ask St. Hippolytus's intercession to put me back together again.

I feel torn. And I think most people in the modern world feel the same way—at least those of us in the first world. This little book addresses three ways that we feel torn and provides short meditations asking God to put us back together.

I feel torn away from living in the present moment by past resentments and future anxieties (part 1). I feel torn away from soothing silence by the constant drum of deafening noise (part 2). I feel torn away from serene stillness by the fast-pace motion, the busyness, the stir-crazy spirit of the world (part 3).

The horses of the past and future, the horses of noise, the horses of busyness are pulling at us every day. It feels that I am present everywhere except the here and now, which is the only place to meet God.

"How was your day, Daddy?" a seven-year-old innocent voice will ask upon my arrival home. Maybe I *feel* too busy to focus on him. Maybe the house seems too chaotic to engage. Or maybe I actually think about my day, remember one miserable moment, and instantly conjure up the bitterness again. In either case, my seven-year-old is ignored.

Sometimes I'm pulled into the distant past to some

harmful moments that gnaw at me. Sometimes I live in the far off future, asking myself the biggest questions: will I outlive one of my twelve children; will I be happy in retirement; will I have any money; will I ever increase in virtue? But more often, I cast myself onto the altar of the near future: will I hit this month's sales goal; do I really have to deal with this person tomorrow; can the kids go to bed an hour early to get them out of my hair?

I should say that I have improved. I have tamed the horses, a bit. When I am conscious of the issue, I can escape the noise, stop the useless movement, and rest in the here and now. But now, I am brutally aware of this fact: most of my problems are self-inflicted. It is as if I strap on the harnesses to the horses myself, bind my hands and feet, and scream, "Hyah!"

As a husband, father, and employer, I have concluded (rightly or wrongly) that those around me suffer mostly due to these wild horses running in different directions. I cannot give someone what I do not have. Thus, I deeply crave to find the serenity of the present moment, of silence, and of stillness so I can share it with those I love.

Saint Hippolytus, please help put me back together again.

PART ONE
THE PRESENT MOMENT

INTRODUCTION TO THE PRESENT MOMENT

Or

Finding the Present Moment Amidst the Storm[2]

"And a great storm of wind arose, and the waves beat into the boat, so that the boat was already filling. But he was in the stern, asleep on the cushion; and they woke him and said to him, 'Teacher, do you not care if we perish?' And he awoke and rebuked the wind, and said to the sea, 'Peace! Be still!' And the wind ceased, and there was a great calm. He said to them, 'Why are you afraid? Have you no faith?' And they were filled with awe, and said to one another, 'Who then is this, that even wind and sea obey him?'" Mark 4:37–41

---

[2] The reader will notice that I quote Mark 4:37–41 in its entirety at the beginning of parts one, two, and three. The reflection for each is similar, but from the standpoint of the present moment, silence, and stillness respectively. I have done this because of the power of the passage. It should speak to us in all three distinct ways—and more.

The chaos of our lives can feel like a great storm of wind. The demands of those with whom we live and work can feel like waves beating against our boat. If we look at the chaos of our lives, we panic, for water is coming in faster than we can bail it out.

And yet Jesus is asleep.

The apostles expected Him to at least help bail water. And yet He was sleeping through the crisis? Imagine their state of mind. Before the storm picked up, they wanted Him to have His rest. He had preached all day. Then the winds became more violent. They were confused at why He would ignore them in this growing crisis. And finally, as the boat began to capsize, they must have grown angry. "Teacher, do you not care if we perish?"

Does the Lord not care when we are beaten by the winds and water of modern times? Does He not care about the storm within our hearts? The stress? The anxiety? Does He not care for His disciples in the modern world who are about to capsize into the sea of despair?

Maybe we understand what the apostles were thinking and feeling.

Jesus, however, awakens and immediately calms the storm. But He looks at them and says, "Why are you afraid? Have you no faith?" And it was the perfect question. It was a perfectly loving rebuke to them, to us.

Jesus was with them in that boat. He was fully present with them, despite seeming not to care about their troubles. The apostles lacked faith in the power of His presence. And so do we.

Jesus is present with us in myriad ways today. He is present most truly in the Blessed Sacrament. He is present in the Scripture. He is present in His Church. He is present in our loved ones. He is even present through our trials and tribulations. Yes, He carries the weight of our cross right next to us.

The Holy Trinity lives in eternity. And our present moment—not our past and not our future—is the closest we can get to eternity. God is as present to us in the present moment as Jesus was to His apostles in that sinking boat.

He can calm our storm any time He wishes. It wouldn't be hard for Him to do. And yet, sometimes He doesn't. Faith teaches us that there is a reason.

We would feel much of the storm subside if we simply embraced Him in the present moment. The answer of faith could be clearer to us. And part one of this little book is about how to do just that.

My Daughter and the Caveman

Or

The Present Moment Is the Most Self-Evident Reality

"Blessed are the pure in heart, for they shall see God." Matthew 5:8

When my first daughter was born, I held her while my wife slept. She was swaddled so tightly and wore a little pink hat. Only her rosy face stuck out. She was perfect.

We shared a recovery room with someone who had the TV on all night. I held Mary Kathleen closely. I apologized to her for being born into a noisy world. And I wondered what she was aware of. Did she hear the TV? Did she miss her mother's heartbeat? Did she recognize my voice?

My philosophical mind went a little deeper: Was she

aware of the past? Was she remembering the traumatic experience of birth? How quickly did she forget the womb? How deep did her thoughts go?

I was in law school when Mary Kathleen was born, and I read a lot on the Founding Fathers of our nation and their notion of "self-evident truths." But how self-evident are self-evident truths? Truths are self-evident if you don't need a bunch of education to understand them—even a caveman can understand them.

The notion that the caveman was a brainless barbarian is not based on any scientific data. The image of them carrying clubs and dragging their women around by the hair is more Hollywood than archeology. The great G. K. Chesterton makes the point that all we know about the caveman is that he was an artist. Whether he painted the walls of his cave for grown men or small babies to enjoy, we do not know. But we know they were artists because we have their art.

We also know that artists think. Imagine: the caveman capturing the running gazelle in a moment, a frozen flash in time. He probably thought about where the gazelle had come from and where it was going. He may have considered the gazelle in a single moment, the "now." He may have considered himself in the now. Maybe the caveman was no longer young enough to go hunting as he did in his past. Maybe the caveman was still young enough to see inside the dimly lit cave. Did he consider his own past and his own future? Did he consider that he was the most real in the present moment, just like the gazelle is in a precise moment? Maybe it is wishful thinking, but I think so.

As Americans, we think about life, liberty, and the pursuit of happiness. But there is an even more self-evident truth that wraps all around us, like a tightly wrapped blanket around a baby.

The present moment is just this. Its origin is not man-made. Its origin lies in God Himself and no other. The present moment is self-evident. It is the one thing that Mary Kathleen understood perfectly at birth. No language is needed; conscious awareness is enough. She did not think about it like me. She did not picture it like the caveman. But she was aware of it; she was in the present moment in a very real way.

If you want to see what the present moment looks like, stare into the eyes of a happy baby.

The present moment is that one phenomenon that everyone, even the world's greatest skeptic, can recognize as existing and present to each of us right now. Whoever denies this is deserving of a straitjacket.

There are other values that are self-evident: love, goodness, and humility, to name a few. The present moment, however, is like a dome of protection holding all self-evident values within it. When the present moment is embraced with a pure heart, all other truths and values come into focus. More importantly, they become easily lived. It is impossible to hate someone while floating atop the soothing waves of the present moment. Why? Because our anger usually comes from the past and our anxiety from the future.

The present moment is where we find peace of mind, joy, and sanctity. I think the caveman would agree. But as a father, I know little children live there, and we must become like these little ones if we are to enter the kingdom of heaven.

Reflection

- The present moment lies beneath all other virtues and sources of happiness. How can I be more aware of this self-evident truth?
- When have I felt that I was stuck in the past or future?
- When in my life have I experienced the present moment as a powerful reality?

ANXIETY ENTERS EDEN

Or

Sin Is the Rejection of the Present Moment

"Cast all your anxieties on him, for he cares about you. Be sober, be watchful. Your adversary the devil prowls around like a roaring lion, seeking some one to devour." 1 Peter 5:7–8

Every time I read a children's Bible to one of my kids, my mind wonders what Eden was really like. Did they lounge around all day? Did they live an ordered and structured life? I know Eden is most likely a literary device to explain a deeper meaning of life before the Fall. I bet it was similar to my own life when I experience great joy in the present moment, whether I am digging a hole or washing dishes. There was the passage of time, but it would have been irrelevant to them. They may have looked at the past and the future, but they did not stare.

In the garden, Adam and Eve lived contentedly, lacking nothing, grateful for everything, in harmony with each other and with God. Each moment was so pure and perfect that no desires drove them to any other state of life. Even their nakedness was as it should be. There was no desire to change or hide or improve. They were fully present in the garden. The sun rose and set, and the earth moved through the heavens, but our first parents existed with great interior silence and stillness as all created things moved about them.

And then, like a bolt of lightning blasting the earth on a beautiful summer day, the serpent, "the most cunning of all the animals," cleverly introduced a foreign concept to the woman's mind. A concept that she had never considered. If she had turned away then, all would have been fine. Curiosity, however, took hold of her, and she continued the discourse with the serpent. Slowly, a new feeling arose in Eve never before felt. Her mind was overwhelmed by this new concept. Her heart was bombarded with a horrific emotion. And then Eve was defeated. She ate the forbidden fruit.

The concept introduced by the serpent was the future. The emotion never felt before was anxiety.

"'For God knows that *when* you eat of it your eyes *will be* opened, and you *will be* like God, knowing good and evil.' So when the woman saw that the tree was good for food, and that it was a delight to the eyes, and that the tree was to be desired to make one wise, she took of its fruit and ate" (Gn 3:5–6, emphasis added).

The serpent placed the notion of the future in Eve's

mind. This knowledge immediately created anxiety in her heart. She felt, for the first time, deprived of something. She felt the future could be better than the present if she broke God's commandment.

The food "was a delight to the eyes." There was a craving to have the fruit. It looked good to eat but not because she was hungry. It looked good because she had not had it before. The food that used to satisfy her now looked stale, boring. She was, for the first time, ill-content, ungrateful, and perhaps angry that something had been withheld from her. The allure of the future was even strong enough to change her sensation of taste. The forbidden fruit spoiled all the food in the garden.

Her new desire went far beyond physical delight. For the first time, she felt the allure of a future state. She had been perfectly content with her knowledge for years. She had taken comfort in her current relationship with God. But that was merely the present. Now she looked on the past as gone. The Eve of yesterday was dull, uninformed, even primitive. She looked with scorn on the past. If she did not take action, the future would be no different. She became anxious about her future state. She feared remaining a simpleton. Would she ever reach her potential? Worse yet, was someone keeping something from her?

She, as the queen of this garden, deserved to be more. The present condition of the garden, perfect in so many ways, was now seen as lacking something. She felt the pull of tomorrow, the promise of something she lacked.

She wanted her eyes to be opened to that which is reserved for God. She wanted more. And more is always in the future. She deserved to know the nature of good and evil. She deserved to be greater tomorrow than she was yesterday.

The more she thought of what was to be, the more she resented her current state. There was so much she did not have. There was so much to be gained. How ignorant she had been before! But wisdom was now hers for the taking. Her mind was filled with both anger about her lowly life and a growing promise of great delight to be had tomorrow. To know the truth of all these hidden realities! To escape the present state of darkness! Her eyes *could be* open. *Could be. Would be. I can be. I must be.* All promises. All lies of the father of lies. All delusions.

The moment Eve left the present moment was the moment she lost intimacy with Adam, even to the point of strapping on fig leaves to hide her nakedness. Yes, the first act of woman after sinning was to create a sexual barrier between herself and her husband, the first act of contraception in human history. She was so discontented with her present state that she had to hide her own body. She desired her body to be something other than it was. The body God gave her was not good enough. There was something more to be had. But that was also in the future. She did not have it now. And so she hid herself, not only from her husband, but from her God. Even as God walked about the garden in the cool of the evening, calling out to her, she felt divorced from Him. The first woman, deluded by prospects of some future state, lost both her husband and her God. Woman is now alone in a brutal world and will forever fight for a future state of life, never satisfied with the present moment.

Reflection

- Do the anxieties of tomorrow pull me away from finding God in the present moment?
- Like Eve, do I feel entitled to "have more"?
- Have my ungodly desires hurt my relationship with my spouse or children? Can living in the present moment help restore these relationships?
- Have I allowed the devil's prowling about my life to devour me with anxiety?

MEETING GOD AT THE RIVER

Or

Prayer Takes You to the Eternal Now

"Draw near to God and he will draw near to you."
James 4:8

"I will pray for you." I say it all the time. People say it to me all the time. I don't believe either happens very often.

I was out to lunch with my mentor and the subject of praying for others came up. He pulled out his daily prayer book, torn to shreds. Since I am in publishing, he asked if I could get it put back together again. He pointed out the litany of names scribbled on the front pages and back, in the margins of different pages, virtually on any white space he could find. "See here," he said, pointing to the names on the back page. "Your name is right here. When I say I will pray for someone, I really do. I pray for them by name." And so he does. I think he is the extreme exception.

I have often confused thinking and praying. I think about thousands of things. I pray for only a few things. This is probably backwards.

Thinking is talking to myself. Praying is talking to God.

Sometimes I am good company, but God always is.

Prayer is a dialogue with God. It is a dialogue that sometimes uses words, sometimes not. Most of the time it seems like a monologue, but I think God speaks back in myriad ways. It is the same with humans. My wife communicates most clearly when she just gives me a look. Words are not needed. It is the same with God. The universe around me is like His face. It gives me certain looks through the eyes of others, through books, through nature, through my own desires. I am by no means a pantheist. But I now find the two-way communication with God far more robust than I used to.

No matter how or when we speak to God, the conversation is smoother when we meet Him where He is. God is in eternity—the *eternal now*. Meeting Him in memories is unreliable. Meeting Him in future projections is presumptuous. And when we use memory or projections, we are thinking rather than praying—talking to ourselves rather than talking to God. Humorously, we can imagine God sitting on His heavenly throne, tapping His finger in boredom, waiting for us to direct our "prayer" to Him rather than ourselves! Prayer can only happen in the present moment.

My prayer life used to be (and sometimes still is) like

a therapist session, as if I am laying on a long couch facing away from the therapist and talking through a stream of consciousness. It was as if I could hear a little "hmm" of affirmation now and then, which encouraged me to keep going. It was sort of a melancholic-adult version of "God bless Mommy and Daddy and Aiden and Mary and Patrick . . ." but filled with drama and complaining and moaning. It was as if the divine therapist was sitting quietly taking notes and simply saying at the end, "I think we should double up our sessions." Why do we need more sessions? You didn't say anything. How is saying nothing for sixty minutes any different from saying nothing for thirty?

I still struggle with this. But I am now conscious of a completely different paradigm. I am now aware of meeting God close to His home; namely, eternity. The present moment is pretty close. It is like coming up to a beautiful river. My present moment is the shore on my side. Eternity is the shore on God's side. I cannot cross over until death carries me across. But I can see across. I can hear across. Just being on the shore brings me peace.

When I pray, I try not to *think* about the past or the future. When someone says, "You will be in my thoughts," I feel like saying, "I don't want to be in your thoughts. Your thoughts are not that impressive. I'd rather be in your prayers." Neither does God wish to meet us in our *thoughts*. He wants to meet in our *prayers*.

Now, when I enter deeper prayer, I try to avoid saying

things like, "I should pray more often," or, "I should do this or that." Those are future thoughts. Any thought beginning with "I should" or "I need" should be used sparingly.[3] Likewise, I limit myself from thinking, "I should have," or, "I should not have." Those are past thoughts. Those are for confession. Maybe I need to say them once to God, but then it's done. God has excellent hearing and an excellent memory. I don't need to grovel before Him.

Rather, I try to simply pray to God in the present moment without any reference of any kind to the future or the past. I have even set my alarm and tried it for five minutes. Of course I fail. But with time, I grow more comfortable just being with God. Actually, I now feel quite silly when I try to convince Him of something. Think about it. The disposition of my heart is all He needs to answer my prayer. Words often screw up the message, like putting a bad melody to a beautiful poem.

Reflection

- Do I confuse thinking and praying?
- Do I use God like a cheap therapist, or do I adore Him as He deserves?

---

[3]   Don't get me wrong: "Lord, I *need* patience" is a great prayer. But here, I am talking more about deeper prayer—contemplation. In contemplation, phrases like "I need" vanish and you end up just being present.

- Which one keeps me in the present: thinking or praying?
- How can I apply the following Scripture passage to my life? "Draw near to God and he will draw near to you" (James 4:8).

SURVIVING A PANIC ATTACK

Or

Free Will Is Only Active In the Present Moment

"Even though I walk through the valley of the shadow of death, I fear no evil; for you are with me; your rod and your staff, they comfort me." Psalms 23:4

I consider myself to have a rather strong constitution. Maybe everyone thinks that. But I can take a punch. I know that. I can work hard for a long time. I know that. And yet I have experienced panic attacks.

I had them when I was a little kid. I called them "the fast things." My mind was racing, my heart was racing, and I was enveloped by an unexplainable fear. My mom took me to the doctor as any good mom would (and she is a great mom). The doctor was convinced I was having nightmares. Nope. I was wide awake. I had the sensation of floating in space or falling out of a race car. All were senses of being out of control at a fast pace. In high school, I self-medicated by punching walls. Stupid. But it worked. The physical pain alleviated the panic, until the next time. As a college student, I medicated with alcohol. But then once I was married and sober, I couldn't hit walls and I couldn't drink. So the panic attacks took a firm grip on me and held me there until they decided to let go—or at least that's what I thought was happening.

I now realize that I personified panic attacks, as if they were something that acted *on* me. And the more I personified "them," the more "they" won. While I can have great sympathy for someone suffering in this way, I now believe it is complete nonsense. I have sympathy for this person like I have sympathy for a man with the compulsion to burn his tongue with a hot iron. I see a sick man hurting himself who really doesn't need to. In fact, I now think of having a panic attack like placing that iron on my tongue. The complete lunacy of that picture helps me get my mind straight.

A panic attack is an odd thing. It is tremendous suffering. It has pushed countless souls to suicide. From my standpoint, it was like being stuck in a vortex of pain that would never end. It was like touching eternity, but in hell rather than in heaven. It was like staring at a clock as the second hand goes slower and slower, and between each second you feel something gripping your soul and squeezing. Maybe that is why breathing is so hard during a panic attack.

Here's the irony: it is not the present moment that is torturous. It is the past and future intruding on the present. The present moment is like Camelot's castle, and the past and future are like barbarians laying siege to all four walls at the same time. You stand in the center of this beautiful fortress and watch an attack from every angle. There is seemingly no escape.

In reality, I did not need an escape. I had no need to leave my castle. I simply had to keep the past resentments and the future anxieties from climbing my walls. So while the panic attack makes you think the present is miserable, the present is in fact your refuge. It is in the present, that billionth of a second between seconds, that serenity is found.

I have not had a panic attack in years precisely because I do not allow the past and future to bombard my castle. I certainly fail at this in small ways throughout the day. But an all-out siege upon my serenity has not occurred in some time.

The present moment is far more real than the past or future. In fact, the past and future only have a theoretical existence due to their dependence on the present moment. That is the problem with personifying fear. It isn't real. It is our own conjuring up of the past and future.

There is a proper way to deal with the past and future. If one remembers the past or conjectures about the future, it must be done while tethered to the present moment. Only then can the mind and soul reach out to grapple with either.

If we come untethered to the present, the past will pull

us down like quicksand. Anger and embarrassment and resentment slowly pull us down. Reliving those moments in our minds hastens the pull, like a desperate man's struggle only sinks him further into quicksand.

Whereas the past slowly sucks us in, the future rips us out of our present moment like a tornado on a clear day. The future breathes on us as a cool breeze. It feels good to plan the solutions to tomorrow's problem or the conversation we will have with the problematic person. But that breeze swirls quickly, and within minutes a funnel forms overhead. Down it comes like a bolt of lightning. There is no way to guard against the velocity at which those future problems swirl. So much debris flies about, ready to take our life at any moment: debris of judgments, self-centered projections on to others, vain aspirations, self-conscious anxiety. If the debris does not take us down, the mere speed of the twister will. Just seconds ago we experienced a light breeze, and now we are trapped in the inescapable funnel of fear and judgment and anxiety. Our feet, which were firmly planted, are now swept off the ground and out of the present.

I am convinced these are the dangers of the past and future. I am convinced these imposters were the stimuli for my own panic attacks. And I am convinced that modern man and woman struggle with this more than any people in history. If only doctors could prescribe silence, stillness, and the present moment.

Reflection

- Do I allow myself to be controlled by fear or anxiety?
- Do I remember that God gave me a free will and that I, in fact, have the power to focus on Him or any other good thing when I so choose?
- Do I truly believe that nothing—NOTH-ING—can rob me of serenity and peace?
- Read the following passage quickly. Then read it slowly. Read it a third time really slowly and consider what God is saying to you: "Even though I walk through the valley of the shadow of death, I fear no evil; for you are with me; your rod and your staff, they comfort me" (Psalms 23:4).

Worse Than a Bullet Wound

Or

You Can Look at the Past. Just Don't Stare.

"Jesus said to him, 'No one who puts his hand to the plow and looks back is fit for the kingdom of God.'"
Luke 9:62

When my son Paul was two years old, we heard him scream upstairs. We have a lot of screams in our busy house, so I paid little attention for the first few seconds. But then the scream seemed different. Something was wrong. I got up and started for the stairs and found my older son carrying Paul to us. Paul was grasping his leg. I looked into his eyes and agony looked back at me. His femur was broken. I've heard that a femur break is worse than a bullet wound, and now I believe it.

His leg was swelling rapidly. I knew that it's possible to bleed to death from femur breaks within minutes due to the large arteries running up your leg. So we made a splint with magazines and Ace bandages, put him on the ironing board like a stretcher, and carried him to the car. We could get to the ER faster than the ambulance could get to us. From the ER, he was taken by ambulance to the local children's hospital.

They could not put his leg in a cast until the swelling went down. So every time he moved, the pain would seize him. He was only two and could not grasp the simple instruction "stay still." They could not give him much pain medication at all. His two-year-old lungs couldn't handle serious pain killers like morphine.

I pulled a chair next to his bed and sat there all night. Every ten minutes a nurse or someone would enter the room and startle him from his sleep, invoking pain all over again.

He suffered deeply.

I suffered deeply. I felt a little like Mary at the foot of the cross.

"Please God! Snap my femur and heal his!" Without question, without hesitation, I would have taken that deal.

I was in one of the finest hospitals in the country, I was sitting right next to him, and I could not do a damn thing. He was too young to soothe with words but old enough to know that I wasn't fixing the problem. For Paul and me, it was a hellish night.

When I think about the painful moments of my past, I can think of teenage events or self-inflicted wounds from drinking or other stupid youthful debacles. I can think of marital disputes in the early days. But I also think of being in the hospital with Paul. When I recall that night, I can hear his cry and see him wince in pain and feel again my own uselessness. The past seems very real to me. I am here and now, but in a sense, I can feel like I am in that hospital six years ago.

It is a painful memory, but I would rather feel it than forget it. Forgetting it would cheapen Paul's suffering—and my own. But how real is the past? I can look at it, but I should never stare.

The past has more objective reality than the future, for the past actually came into being. It also went out of being. It is no more. It is vapor, but vapor is something that is the remnant of something else, like memory itself.

The past has lasting effects on the present moment. Our actions have consequences, for good or evil. We learn from the past. We repent for past behavior. But we cannot relive it. Such a statement sounds obvious. Why, then, do I allow old feelings to resurface ten or twenty years later? I remember Paul in the hospital. There is something healthy in this since the memory represents my love for him. But why do I play out old scenarios of defeats and victories in my mind? I think most people do this, especially white-collar folks. Blue collar people are often working with their bodies so much that they don't have time to live in the past. White collar people need more medication because they have time to be self-centered. So much for money bringing comfort . . .

The past is dangerous because it is usually relived as either resentment or nostalgia, both intruders on the present truth. A healthy memory is good. But an unhealthy memory is one that captures your mind and begins to bend it. My memory of Paul helps me love him more today. Other memories—especially ones that I stare at—have the opposite result.

And this is where resentment comes into play.

Reflection

- Do I distinguish between healthy and unhealthy memories?
- Do I relive dangerous moments from my past?
- Can I entrust the past to God and simply be with Him in the present?
- Scripture says, "Jesus said to him, 'No one who puts his hand to the plow and looks back is fit for the kingdom of God'" (Luke 9:62). Why is Jesus telling you to not look back when you are trying to move the plow forward?

A FORTY-YEAR BLEED

Or

Resentment Means "to Re-Feel"

"Let all bitterness and wrath and anger and clamor and slander be put away from you, with all malice."
Ephesians 4:31

I was sitting across the table from a friend. He told me a story from nearly forty years ago. As he spoke, the anger welled up. If someone had walked up to us at that moment, they would have thought the injury done to him forty years ago had just happened. My mind was playing double duty: I was both listening to the story and marveling at how quickly old feelings came back to his heart and old tapes replayed in his mind. He was mutilating himself from the inside out, for he relived these memories regularly—a forty-year-old wound he refused to let heal. I wondered if there was a way to remember the painful experience without reliving it. Would the bleeding ever stop? If only bad memories could be amputated.

Resentment is a wonderful word. It derives from the Latin *sentire*, meaning "to feel." Resentment means to "re-feel," usually referring to bad feelings. Why do we want to relive bad feelings? The more we do it, the more we relish it. It becomes familiar, like worn leather. We fail to embrace the freshness of the present moment and fall back on the familiar feelings of the past, like a homeless man who would rather sleep on the floor than in a comfortable bed. We become addicted to damaging ourselves with our past.

Old thoughts and feelings are more addictive than heroin. And the sensation is similar. I heard a guy once say nothing feels worse than heroin the first time and nothing feels better than heroin the hundredth time. The sensation of pain is the greatest pleasure. Here is the simple reason cigarette smoking is so difficult to quit. People are addicted to easing the pain every few hours more than they are to actual nicotine. The more we embrace the pain and ease it, the more we need it.

But the most treacherous of all addictions are those of memories. Mental memories are bad. Appetitive memories—memories of the appetites—are even worse. I can change or redirect your mind in a flash. I would just walk you through a math problem. But changing your appetites, your passions, especially habitual responses to stimuli, is a monumental feat.

Aristotle called us habitual animals. We learn to navigate through the world with habits. Your eyes learned the habit of reading left to right. Your legs learned the habit of walking. Your lungs learned the habit of breathing smoothly. And your passions have learned the habit of feeling certain sensations over and over again.

So many of us operate daily like an insane person, walking an endless circle around haunted nooks and crannies of the mind, knowing a villain awaits us within. We may do our job and carry on conversations and stop at red lights, but within, we are playing the same bad movie in our mind over and over again. We are usually the victims. And with every passing blow, we suffer, we increase our need to feel it again.

Reflection

- Do I dwell on old feelings and old memories?
- Do I play the role of the martyr in my mind?
- Do I rationalize or justify these negative feelings because they are internal and not outwardly spoken?

Breaking Pencils

Or

You Can Look at the Future. Just Don't Stare.

"Do not be anxious about tomorrow, for tomorrow will be anxious for itself. Let the day's own trouble be sufficient for the day." Matthew 6:34

We have always homeschooled our kids. We did all the right things—so we thought. My wife taught our first kid, Aiden, phonics over and over again. He really struggled with reading at every grade level. He could barely write. We doubled down on the writing assignments. We had him memorize spelling lists. Torture. He clearly didn't seem to be a visual learner, but he didn't seem to remember the spelling of words either. "Kinesthetic learner," I figured. So I did spelling lists with him while throwing the baseball. Aiden has a great throwing arm and still can't spell to save his life.

Finally, when he was twelve, we got a full battery of tests. He was dyslexic, and pretty extreme at that. He was highly intelligent, conversed with the tester like no other student, but had all the signs of dyslexia. We just didn't know what to look for. He was our lab rat, as every first kid is.

When the doctor explained the severity of the case, my mind shot forward twenty years in the future. Can he ever be a lawyer, like me? Can he ever be a writer, like me? Can he ever be a publisher, like me? Will he love books, like me?

There were at least three problems with these thoughts. First, I was comparing him to me. That's just stupid. Second, I did not understand the unusual gifts he had that far, far make up for the deficiency in perceiving character shapes. Third, and most deceptively, I was way off in the future. Did Aiden need to apply to law school today? Did he need to write a book or be a publisher today? Did he need to sit on the back deck of his house in the early morning with a cup of coffee and enjoy a book today?

All of my concerns were for his future. And largely, they were silly questions about his future. I should have been concerned with what he needed *now*. The doctor said to Ashley and me, "The only problem here with this disability is going to be Conor." Wait. What? "You need to go home and break the pencils with Aiden. Liberate him from this ball and chain. There is another way for him to learn. And you will either help him or get in his way. It's your choice."

After I cooled my jets, I trusted him. We went home. Aiden and I broke the pencils.

I became focused on learning about dyslexia, helping Aiden get through his current schoolwork while protecting his self-image. From then on, I refused to let my mind wander off into the distance. I found ways in the here and now for him to learn as much as possible and to love learning. We got him audio books, a laptop, and dictation software. We picked classes (college courses actually) that he could listen to or watch. We slightly altered the way he was tested.

The result is that Aiden is the best-read teenager I have ever met. His love of literature and history dwarfs my own. He has processed more books through audio then I ever will with my eyes. The anxiety I felt was utterly useless. But this is exactly the way the devil wants it.

"In a word, the Future is, of all things, the thing least like eternity. It is the most completely temporal part of time—for the Past is frozen and no longer flows, and the Present is all lit up with eternal rays" (*Screwtape Letters*, Bk XV).

Thinking about the future is one of the trademarks of humanity. It is what tells me to have a lot of life insurance—especially with twelve kids. Apes can build a small structure to grab the banana, but they will not consider how their young will eat bananas after their death or how future generations will find sufficient banana resources.

Their future is limited to a season at best, and this is driven more by instinct, like geese flying south for the winter.

Mankind, however, embarks on its greatest endeavors with *only* future generations in mind. Those fifty- and sixty-year-olds working on putting a man on Mars today know it will not happen during their career and probably not in their own lifetime. This does not dissuade the power of dreams.

Our Founding Fathers knew that much of the Constitution would not be applicable until future generations. But they were capable of feeling the duty to set forth timeless principles that would outlive them.

And yet our greatest virtues are often the flip side of our greatest vices.

It is our unique power to keep the future before our eyes that, more than anything else, causes us to abandon the present moment. The future pulls us away from the only spot that eternity touches earth. The future, as Screwtape said, is where the devil wants us.

By definition, the future is uncertain. Humans do not handle uncertainty well. I handle it horribly. It gives us anxiety, a crippling disease that plagues modern man. Christ said, "Do not be anxious about tomorrow, for tomorrow will be anxious for itself. Let the day's own trouble be sufficient for the day" (Mt 6:34). Christ is not saying to forgo plans or not make arrangements or recognize future threats to safety. He is, however, saying that worrying about it (beyond that of making reasonable plans) is a lack of faith in God. "And which one of you by being anxious can add one cubit to his span of life?" (Mt 6:27).

In other words, it is alright to look at the future; just don't stare at it.

Stress is at an all time high, particularly in white-collar communities. Doctors are prescribing mood-altering drugs at astonishing rates just so soccer moms can get through the afternoon with their own children. Most of this stress is due to worrying about the future, however petty the concern may be. What will this person say to me? Will my kid get into Chapel Hill? Can we afford the beach house? How will I ever lose weight? What will retirement be like being with my husband all day?

Asking questions is like taking medications. They must be asked at the right time and in the right amount. You can no more answer a question by pouring on the worry than you can cure an infection by drinking the entire bottle of antibiotics.

Stress is thinking about something when you don't want to.

Most questions are not crippling in themselves. But they drain us of mental energy, of spiritual joy, of familial affection when we allow them to trespass on restricted areas of our lives.

Anxiety about the future rips us from the soil of the present we are planted in. It is only in the present moment that we can produce fruit. And just as fruit requires the roots of its tree to absorb water and nutrients from deep within the ground, so too can spiritual fruit only result from our being deeply rooted in the present moment. Our nutrients and hydration are never found in the past or in the future.

There is an element of pride in our worrying about the future. We are looking into the abyss of what is yet to come and trying to give it shape and form and language, and then trying to vanquish it. There is something God-like in seeing what is to come. There is something God-like in giving it shape and form. And just as God creates us in His image and likeness, so do we create the future (in our minds) in our image and likeness. We rarely make ourselves the villain in our future fantasies. We are usually the victim, the martyr. We incarnate ourselves in the future world, always on innocent and humble terms. And we project that we will be scorned, mocked, abused. And we are an unblemished lamb led to the slaughter.

It is very hard for us creatures, who fell in the garden due to a twisted desire to be like God, to create a future scenario in our minds that rightly reflects our own shortcomings. We instead place ourselves in the most positive light possible. This is the natural consequence of pride.

In the present moment, however, we are not as prideful. We give ourselves a more honest look. When we embrace the present, we more humbly admit our sins. The present does not allow room for fiction. But when we project into the future, something in our subconscious says that we will make huge moral improvements—we will be a completely different person—by the time the future arrives. This psychological phenomenon explains why it is so easy to start diets tomorrow. Today we know we lack self-control over the late-night snack. But by tomorrow, we will conjure up the strength—we will finally get serious—about our commitment. It is as if will-power will grow over night. Fat and fungus grow overnight. Not will-power.

I hate conversing with someone who is lost in the future. They are not even listening to you, even though they nod and smile. It is offensive, and it should be. And when they talk, they talk past you. I'm guilty. I've done it. And the problem isn't just that it is rude or unproductive. More importantly, when I do this, I fail to recognize the other person's value in the here and now.

This is especially problematic in a household of so many kids. They all want to talk to me. I eventually tune out. I give a lot of "hmm" and grunts of affirmation, but I'm not really listening.

I have found that gathering myself, focusing intently on the child for a minute or less, hearing everything they are trying to say (they often don't have the right words), and trying to give meaningful responses makes the conversation much shorter. When I'm not listening, they know it and keep talking. When I do listen, they feel satisfied, checking it off their own mental list, and run along. It is the same with a wife. It is the same with employees. It is the same with everyone. A little focus goes a long way.

And yet our troubled modern world is so replete with distracted individuals—usually lost in the virtual reality of email and social media—that one person is too distracted to even be offended. Two adults, both lost in the delusions of the future or groveling in the resentments of the past, are not overtly offended by the other because neither was really paying attention to the other in the first place. It is like two strangers passing in the night. Only shadows are visible, for the mind and heart of each—the real person—is hardly present. A phantom of the real self is all one has access to.

It is critical to our well-being and eternal salvation to stay out of the future as much as possible. The future is full of empty promises and empty threats, both of which drain our soul of peace and joy in the present.

Sometimes we must break the pencils that we think will write a perfect future.

Reflection

- Do we project our own future ideas onto those we love?
- Read this passage once quickly. Then once slowly. Then a third time really slowly. "Do not be anxious about tomorrow, for tomorrow will be anxious for itself. Let the day's own trouble be sufficient for the day" (Mt 6:34). What is God saying to you?

The Magic of Mason Jars

Or

Children, Nature and the Present Moment

"Truly, I say to you, unless you turn and become like children, you will never enter the kingdom of heaven." Matthew 18:3

My aunt and uncle lived in the country when I was a child. Their house was lined with rock walls and every type of flower and plant imaginable. My aunt had the greenest thumb you ever saw. Upon arrival at their house, I would race to the rock walls and look for lizards. They were everywhere. I would gently push back flowers and search the soil beneath them. I could spend hours searching the cracks and crevices of the rock wall. Even though I was looking for lizards, I loved getting up close to the flowers. My aunt would come outside and tell me the names of every plant I came to. I had no desire to memorize the names, but I loved the sound of her voice saying them. To this day, when I think of a peaceful

45

domestic setting, I think of rock walls, flowers, lizards, and an older lady with a green thumb who knows the names of everything.

My kids have only met this aunt once. And it wasn't at her house. By then, the house was gone. They moved to a retirement home far away. My kids met her in a simple townhome. Nothing spectacular from nature's standpoint. She was with my kids for maybe an hour. And the entire time, Aunt Bonnie took them on a nature walk.

Outside the front door, there were a few potted plants and some bushes. There was a small tree. She led my kids by their hands around this tiny front yard. She pointed out every living thing. She told them their names. She told them how they were planted. She told them God made them. She told them how they ate and drank and grew. She taught them how to pick a few tiny yellow flowers that were growing in the grass, some purple plants that were tucked behind some bushes, some green weeds.

The kids came in with their hands full. She grabbed a few old Mason jars, put some water in them, and showed the kids how to carefully decorate that Mason jar with each plant. The kids were filled with joy. The picture I still have of them smiling with their great-aunt and their Mason jar masterpieces reminds me of their experience with Aunt Bonnie and my own, looking for lizards.

My home today is much different than Aunt Bonnie's. For most moderns, our twelve children must seem less a family than a tribe, and having a tribe together under one roof makes our house a noisy, rambunctious, distracting place. When the distractions grate deeply, when I am ready to permanently banish televisions and laptops and battery-operated toys from our walls and decree a perpetual Great Silence from dawn to dusk, I try instead to take the little kids on a nature walk, like Aunt Bonnie would do.

Once upon a time, when I scoured through the rock walls, I understood how to take a nature walk. I forgot. Somewhere along the line, I forgot this sacred knowledge. I began moving only for a purpose. Utilitarianism took hold of me as it does most people, especially Americans with a protestant work ethic. When I am outdoors and moving, I am reaching for a goal: two miles or half a marathon, two hundred or two thousand burned calories, to fix the fence or to pick up the trash. But I have begun to let my kids teach me how to take a walk. Slowly but surely, I am learning again to see what they see.

My five-year-old is free from such silly goals. Imelda walks for the enjoyment of each second. With each second comes another bug to look at, another crack in the sidewalk to follow, another flower to smell, another stone to skip, another wall to climb, and, if I am lucky, a lizard to chase. Mileage and calories mean nothing.

Every parent and grandparent can entertain small children for hours by simply taking them on a nature walk. All that is needed is a little nature. Every tree is a miracle to explore. Look up and see how the trees lean toward the sunlight and animals of all kinds take refuge in their branches. Look down and see how roots spread about the ground like a beautiful tapestry of a master weaver. Look straight ahead and see how the bark defends the tree like body armor. And then let the child tell you how this tree is a gift from God, not only providing shelter for the birds of the air, but for us as well.

Imelda can tell me she rests under its shade, like the birds. She now knows she lives in a house and sits on a chair and eats from tables made with its wood. She knows she can draw pictures for mommy with pencils carved from its limb. Imelda meets this single tree in the present moment and is better prepared to face the future, no matter what it brings.

Children live in the present.

Adults are filled with resentment or nostalgia of the past and anxiety about the future. Children have very little past to resent and few anxieties to pull them into the future. This is why children suffer so much better than adults. It is very common for a child dying of cancer to approach it as a saint. The littlest suffering souls accept each day as it comes. They look at the future, but do not stare. They shrug their shoulders and move on.

Children live in the present because they marvel at the splendor of creation. They are grateful for the smallest acts of kindness. They look for immediate ways to bring joy to others. They are very busy taking in all the present stimuli: their parents' love, their siblings' fun and games, the beauty all around them.

And yet how do we try to entertain children? We give them iPads and video games. As the battery powers up, the child powers down. Their soul is put on airplane mode, running on minimal power, with no awareness of the natural beauties around them.

I think we adults do this with children for a few reasons. First, we think it is easier for us. Second, and most difficult to believe, misery loves company. Something deep in our subconscious desires to justify the countless hours we spend as a zombie in front of the screen. And subjecting the young and innocent to the same condition tells us that it cannot be all that bad.

Another way that children embrace the present moment is how they engage with other human beings. Whereas adults are often like phantoms of the night, passing by each other in a fog of distraction, a child approaches you with wide eyes, awake and ready, fully present, fully expecting to speak to you with energy and passion. And their little hearts can be broken, for time after time they are met with a mother or father lost in the cell phone, giving only cursory nods and grunts pretending to engage.

G. K. Chesterton said, "Angels can fly because they take themselves so lightly." The same is true for a child's spirit. Just as children's bodies are nimble enough to throw themselves about without pulling a muscle, their spirits are light enough to be lifted high by the joy of the moment. They can throw themselves into whatever they are doing. They are not tethered, held back, restrained by the past, and they are not distracted by the future.

A child is contemplative. They need not contemplate like adults do, often withdrawn from the world. They need not withdraw precisely because they are so *in* the world. They are not *of* the world, as we say. The world has not rubbed off on them yet. But they are *in* the cracks and crevices of this beautiful world like lizards hiding in Aunt Bonnie's rock wall.

A child focuses with great intensity on each and every item he encounters in the present moment. Again, see that young child on a walk. His spirit joins with each object along the way. The destination is irrelevant. As the Trappist monk says, "Contemplation is doing one thing." And this child is doing one thing fully and completely along the way, one after the other, each thought unencumbered by the past and future.

Children listen to the world. They hear the beautiful things of life calling their name. I wish I could be like Aunt Bonnie, calling out the names of beautiful things to my children, helping them be on a first name basis.

Reflection

- How have I allowed the modern world to ruin my childlike spirit?

- Do I foster or harm my children's natural love for nature and the present moment?
- How is God speaking to me through the following verse? "Truly, I say to you, unless you turn and become like children, you will never enter the kingdom of heaven" (Matthew 18:3).

THE ELEVENTH INNING

Or

Sports and the Present Moment

"A cheerful heart is a good medicine." Proverbs 17:22

It was the sixth game of the 2011 World Series. The Rangers were winning the series 3-2 against the Cardinals. We were Cardinals fans, and they had a two-run deficit (7-5) in the bottom of the ninth inning. Two runners were on base. David Freese was at bat with a 1-2 count. The Rangers were literally one strike away from winning the World Series. It was sad to watch your team approach the end. My nine-year-old, Aiden, and I were glued to the TV. He had dozed off a few times during the game, but now was wide awake. Then, something magical happened.

David Freese got a pitch right down the middle and hit a triple to the right field wall, driving in both runners. It was hard to believe.

Extra innings.

The Rangers scored two runs in the top of the tenth. Our hearts were broken, as again, the Rangers were one strike away from winning the World Series. And then, something magical happened again. Our Cardinals erased the deficit with two runs. Unbelievable. At this point, we knew the Cardinals had to win. Destiny would not let the Rangers get that last strike—twice.

Into the eleventh inning.

I began to notice Aiden as much as the Cardinals. He was fully alive in the present moment. Nothing else mattered. He was relentlessly focused. His mind and passions were honed to the tip of an arrow, with precision that a Marine sniper wishes he had. I think the ball even slowed down in his mind so he could savor every millisecond. Aiden was in the present moment. I remember wondering how he might do in math if the same level of precision was brought to his textbook. What would his mother say if he cleaned his room with the same intensity?

Adults, too, become most childlike when they are playing or watching sports. The great Fr. James Schall says, "I will argue something . . . that may sound like a rather startling theory, but held with tenacity. I want to suggest that the closest the average man ever gets to contemplation in the Greek sense is watching a good, significant sporting event, be it the sixth game of the World Series, the European Cup soccer finals, the center court at

Wimbledon, or the county championships of his daughter's volleyball team" (*On the Seriousness of Sports*).

An avid golfer, who fritters away a good deal of life, can often tell you every stroke of every player over eighteen holes. An avid football fan, who cannot see the overt body language in his wife and children, can spot the slightest penalty amidst the chaotic movement of twenty-two men on a field.

The present moment converts normal humans into super humans every day. Remarkable feats are possible that defy human physiology. The present moment enables every neuron and muscle fiber to engage in perfect harmony. The results are staggering. And yet we willfully throw ourselves into the past and future, abandoning the present moment as if it is boring.

Time stands still because the present contains everything within itself. It is not pulling the past along with it nor pushing the future into reality. It is wholly and completely subsistent within itself.

It is the bottom of eleventh inning. David Freeze steps up to the plate again. He had three balls and two strikes, a full count. He swings. The ball towers over the center field wall, going far more than four hundred feet. My son next to me went wild! And he introduced me to the present moment.

Reflection

- Have I experienced "time standing still" in sports? How would I explain the phenomenon?

- Consider what Fr. Schall said: "I want to suggest that the closest the average man ever gets to contemplation in the Greek sense is watching a good, significant sporting event . . ." What does this tell you about prayer?

- How might I better focus on my daily life in order to squeeze the maximum potential out of it?

THE MARRIAGE REVELATION

Or

When God Speaks, Time Stands Still

"He made the storm be still, and the waves of the sea were hushed." Psalms 107:29

She was wearing a blue dress. Her hands were folded in front of her. I was standing on gravel. I could feel it shift beneath me, not sure if my knees were wobbling. The cathedral stood tall behind me. I felt like it was hovering all around me, whispering in my ear, pushing me forward. She looked at me with stillness, a lady, waiting to be addressed.

I gave one of those gestures with my hand, like I was coming to say something. I didn't know what to say. Time stood still. Her face, her hair, her blue dress and blue eyes, her slight smile, her folded hands—everything instantly burned into my soul. It was a third-degree burn. It hurt. It was like God took a branding iron from His heavenly furnace and pressed it against my soul, leaving an indelible mark.

Don't ask me how, but I knew it was over. My previous life was over. A new life began with that indelible mark on my soul. Baptism by fire. I would marry her. I knew it. Don't ask me how.

I did just that three years later. If the customs and expectations of the world were not in my way, I would have married her three minutes later. It would have been easier, for sure. It was like a piece of that gravel got stuck in my shoe for three years. Every step hurt.

For a thinker, the worst thing that time gives is more time to think. More thoughts on something I already know become self-poison. Very little is accomplished except trouble when I overthink. There is nothing worse than discerning that which needs no discernment. But the world says, "Take your time." Maybe so, but try saying that to a drowning man. Try saying that to a man being chased by a bear. Allegedly, relaxing is the way to survive, but you can't blame the poor guy for panicking.

There was a perfect silence and stillness in that moment as I stood between her and the cathedral. I had not even heard her voice. Superfluous. I did not know her name. Superfluous.

Science has now captured the moment of conception on camera. There is an explosion, a burst of light. It is the fireworks of God's rejoicing. I think the sacraments are something like this—a metaphysical nuclear bomb, eternity breaking into time. And I think sacramental moments are something like this. I felt a metaphysical explosion in my soul, for eternity broke into my time. No wonder my knees wobbled.

Finally, the smoke cloud settled. I had to say something. I said the best thing I could come up with. "Hi." It felt like I couldn't speak, a silent hermit coming forth from years of seclusion. "Hi" was all my voice box could handle.

Time stood still.

Reflection

- What has been the most powerful moment in my life? Was God present?
- How will I know the next powerful moment in my life when it occurs?
- Has God ever given me a profound intuition as a gift?

PART TWO
SILENCE

INTRODUCTION TO SILENCE

Or

Finding Silence Amidst the Storm

"And a great storm of wind arose, and the waves beat into the boat, so that the boat was already filling. But he was in the stern, asleep on the cushion; and they woke him and said to him, 'Teacher, do you not care if we perish?' And he awoke and rebuked the wind, and said to the sea, 'Peace! Be still!' And the wind ceased, and there was a great calm. He said to them, 'Why are you afraid? Have you no faith?' And they were filled with awe, and said to one another, 'Who then is this, that even wind and sea obey him?'" Mark 4:37–41

The winds howled and the waves thrashed against the boat. Everyone was yelling to hold the lines or bail the water. The mere sounds of the chaos are enough to make your heart pound.

Each of the apostles likely heard not only the external

noise around him but also his inner voice screaming countless thoughts. "I knew that storm was coming this way!" "Why didn't the others listen to me?" "I can barely see!" "I'm exhausted!" "I don't want to die!" "Jesus is ignoring us!" The hearts of the apostles moved faster than the fastest gust of wind.

As do our own hearts. How often we allow our trials and fears to affect our peace!

To survive any crisis, we must learn to embrace the silence that lives between the many noises in our lives. Not only must we look for moments of external silence—away from the insane amount of deafening noise all around—but we must also find that internal silence, even when our boats are about to capsize.

God desires to speak to us in the silence of our heart, just as He spoke to the storm: "Peace. Be still." Only if we can reach that place of silence residing deeply in our soul—only if we can search for God in that silent world within—will we ever hear amidst the storm that still small voice: "Peace. Be still." Part two of this little book attempts to explain how to do just that.

ANGELS SING SILENCE

Or

Silence Is Not the Absence of Noise

"A spirit glided past my face; the hair of my flesh stood up." Job 4:15

My thirteen-year-old daughter walked on stage. She wore a beautiful green dress. I noticed for the first time that she looked more like a woman than a girl. The room was hushed. Mary approached the microphone. I anxiously awaited to hear her singing voice since she had refused up to then to sing in front of me. I then noticed, right before the accompaniment began, with a quiet crowd and my beautiful daughter staring out into the crowd, that silence had enveloped the room.

The silence was palpable. It was real. It was not the absence of noise. It was something very closely tied to the present moment. Her beauty and innocence were in perfect harmony with the silence. I could have sat there forever.

Mary was so present. There was no distraction. Nothing catching my eye to the left or right. No thoughts were pulling me to the past or the future. It was as if angels were singing the silence as a prelude to Mary's song.

At this point in my life, I was already enamored with the topic of the present moment. I had read a few books on the topic of silence. But now I understood them together, staring at my daughter silently standing on a stage.

Silence is a fraternal twin to the present moment. They are birthed directly from eternity, though they are not identical. I appreciate the notion of fraternal twins because I have them. It is a funny thing. There was two in one. Same nine months. Same ultrasounds. Same hospital bills. But two distinct individuals, and yet forever linked in a way few people ever are.

What is silence? Is it just the air all about when you can hear a pin drop? Is it just the absence of noise? No. I sensed something real when my daughter looked out over the crowd.

Silence, rather, is a foundational reality that lies beneath all we experience in the present moment. It is fertile soil from which beautiful sound arises: words of truth, the laughter of children, the singing voice of a daughter you love.

Truth and beauty expressed through sound are like ornaments hanging on silence. The beauty of the sound is in direct correlation to its interconnection with the silence from which it sprung. If the sound abandons silence, if it violently shatters silence, the sound itself will lose cohesion. It will morph into deafening noise, like a high pitch breaking glass. Noise—as opposed to sound—has no connection with the present moment. Noise is the auditory phenomenon of past and future intruders breaking into the present moment.

And when she opened her mouth and sang, the angels' song of silence did not cease. They wrapped her notes in their wings and brought them to me.

Reflection

- How is the present moment and silence closely related?
- Have I grown numb to the noise all around me?
- St. Teresa of Calcutta said, "In the silence of the heart God speaks." What does this mean to me?

THE HARDEST PENANCE EVER

Or

Silence Is Where We Can Experience the Dialog of Love Between the Father and the Son

"Even a fool who keeps silent is considered wise; when he closes his lips, he is deemed intelligent."
Proverbs 17:28

I went to confession to a young priest and confessed not wanting to pray. At that point in my life, I was working hard and I was frustrated with everything. Prayer seemed like an utter waste of time, though I knew better and confessed.

The priest gave me the harshest penance I have received. It was about 7 pm at night. "For your penance, I want you to go to Eucharistic Adoration right now—if at all possible—and stay there until you want to be there."

I thought this priest was out of his mind. Now that

the priest is older and more experienced, I wonder if he would give such a penance. Maybe.

I called home and told my wife I was going to adoration (and did not volunteer that it was a penance). I got to the chapel, settled into a chair, and said, "OK, Jesus, I want to be here. Time to go." But my conscience wouldn't let me get up. "OK, Jesus. A part of me wants to be here. See you later." I couldn't move. Dang it. I can't just fake this. I gotta do it right. I concentrated so hard on wanting to be there that the old lady next to me must have thought I was sick to my stomach. "DANG IT! Want to be here! Want to be here!" Would I be here all night? Would I starve to death in three days?

For over an hour, I was tortured with solving this problem. Finally, I settled. Slowly, I stopped trying. I prayed for my wife and children back home. I prayed that I would have greater gratitude than I had. I prayed I would be a better husband and father. I prayed for perseverance in prayer. I prayed for humility. I prayed for a greater awareness of the True Jesus right in front of me. And I finally sat quietly, hoping the Father or the Son would speak to me. Finally, I shut up. Finally, I listened.

I did not hear a voice. But I had an awareness that God the Father communicated with God the Son in a way I could not understand. I wanted to hear this communication between the Father and the Son. I wanted to hear how they spoke to the Holy Spirit. I wanted to be in that Trinitarian life.

And then I realized I wanted to be there. It was then that I was ready to go home to my family. My penance was fulfilled.

Silence is where we can experience the dialog of love between the Father and the Son. The perfect unity between them allows complete and unencumbered truth and love to flow back and forth, communicating all that they are to each other. Silence is the channel for the exchange. A spoken word would break this silence. It would introduce a small division in the perfect flow between them. It would be like a hiccup in the climax of a beautiful song.

But there is the Word. The Word was God. The Word is God. He did not become the Word in the Incarnation but was eternally begotten of the Father. This Word is the perfect word because it never breaks the silence. This Word never divides the speaker from the speech. This Word is not a piece of God broken out to live on its own. It is, rather, eternally begotten in silence and the present moment. All of the Father's truth and goodness and beauty emanate through this Word.

And the Word became flesh and dwelt among us. The Word came into the world with as much silence as this earth can foster. His mother was the "woman wrapped in silence."

It is in silence with God that our desire for Him grows. It was the worst penance. It was the best penance.

Reflection

- If I could hear the dialog between the Father and Son, what would I hear?
- Do I talk God's ear off?
- How does this Proverb apply to me? "Even a fool who keeps silent is considered wise; when he closes his lips, he is deemed intelligent"(Proverbs 17:28).

Yoga Yuppies at Starbucks

Or

The Difference Between Speech and Chatter

"Set a guard over my mouth, O LORD, keep watch over the door of my lips!" Psalms 141:3

I was recently doing some work at Starbucks. Two women in their yoga outfits were talking. Well, maybe I should not go so far as to say "talking." All I heard was chatter.

The voice inflections were the affectations of *prima donnas*. I had heard it many times before. I live near a yuppie community. It is par for the course. I tried not to eavesdrop. But the noise coming from the two women was too painful to ignore.

The subject of chatter was about how other people did not appreciate how busy their schedules were (note: it was mid-morning in the middle of the week and they had just left yoga class together and were enjoying lattes). The listener responded with furrowed brow and pretentious moans of affirmation but was only awaiting her own chance to one-up her friend. I heard a few "Oh my God!" artificial expressions of disgust at the villain behind the story. There was a valley girl tone to that "Oh my God!" Two sins were present: breaking the second commandment and using such an obnoxious voice inflection. The first is objectively worse, but the second should be punishable by death.

These two chatterers had nothing to say, and they knew it. They both suffered from a severe case of "up talk": when you raise your tone and accentuation at the end of the phrase, unintentionally revealing your insecurity. Up talk is a cataclysm of the modern world.

In the coffee shop, the chatter ended with each woman saying how they now had to enter back in to their world of unfairness and suffering. They made a fake plan to reconnect, always having to leave the setting with a posturing of proficiency. I considered pouring my steaming-hot coffee all over myself to feel better but didn't want to waste my five dollars.

Each got in their car and drove away, surely lacking any rejuvenation. Most assuredly, the anxiety they expressed was merely heightened. The act of bloviating for sixty minutes over coffee is not therapeutic. It is treating the illness with the disease. I suspect the problem was compounded. I also suspect one or both of them regularly visit their doctor for mood altering drugs for depression and anxiety. Such is the modern world. I felt sorry for them, but only for a second. I realized that selfishness and self-centeredness can come in many forms. What I then focused on was whether my children would grow up and discourse with others like that. Have I taught them to talk? Sure, I've taught them vocabulary and grammar and how to string words together. I have tried to root out the word *like* from that vocabulary, and I ruthlessly make them repeat sentences without up talk. But do I teach them to truly engage with the other person while talking?

Here is the relation of chatter to silence: chatter comes out of silence as puss from a boil. There is an infection in the soul that grows and must ooze out. Eventually the infection comes out of the human mouth. "And he called the people to him and said to them, 'Hear and understand: not what goes into the mouth defiles a man, but what comes out of the mouth, this defiles a man'" (Mt 15:10–11).

I contrast this with true communication. There are many examples, but I recall one more than any other. The deepest conversation I ever had included a total of four words. I was on my knees at the communion rail in St. Peter's Church in Steubenville, OH. I reached in my pocket, pulled out a small box, turned my head toward Ashley, and said, "Will you marry me?" She said, "Yes." Now *that* was communication. A lifetime of mutual commitment was said in a total five words.

When two people speak from the depths of their souls with meaning and focus, both silence and the present moment are wrapped around them. Silence and the present moment shroud them from time.

We have all experienced time standing still. We have experienced watching sports or staring in the eyes of our first love. We can experience it regularly in deep conversation with a true friend. Time stands still when two souls wrap around each other, spiral upward toward heaven, and touch eternity. Those two imposters, past and future, are of little importance. They may talk about things of the past or future, but their souls are united in the present.

True conversation embraces both silence and the present moment. It is like the present moment is a boulder plunged into the sea of silence. Noise of the past and future are splashed away as the boulder sinks deeper and deeper into the present moment.

But when we merely chatter (that is, speech devoid of true purpose), the present moment slips away. This chatter is like a razor thin stone that skims across the past and future. There is no weight, no substance to this engagement. Nothing goes deep. It skips and skips, never making a real impact. And you say things like, "Oh my God!" with valley girl inflection.

A human that merely chatters is offensive to human nature. He is like a fish that can't swim or a bird that can't fly. Chatter violates the very core of what makes us human.

Aristotle says man is a rational animal, *zoon logon echon*. He also explains that this rationality is mostly evidenced by our ability to speak rather than howl or grunt.

Logos is a Greek word with numerous translations, including "meaning," "reason," and "word." Christ was the *Logos* of the Father. Our words are our meaning, our rationality. And thus we are *zoon politikon*, political animals, animals that get things done in society by speaking.

Our nature requires that we express ourselves through the word. Much of what is in us must come out. A silent hermit uses interior words to speak with God. Man must express himself. If he is empty of truth and goodness, his mouth will still open and he will make noise. Some people just scream and call it music.

Modern man cannot stay quiet for a single day. Consider for yourself: when was the last time you did not speak to anyone for a single day? Most people cannot string more than a few hours together (during their waking hours) when they do not communicate with someone in person, on the phone, in an email, by texting, or through social media.

We are addicted to chatter. It is nervous energy. It is hyperactivity of the soul. It is fear of silence, for silence shines a great light on the truths we choose to ignore.

When two people chatter, the virtue of charity is lacking. It is replaced by self-centeredness and self-righteousness. The ability to listen, the ability to focus on the other's chatter in search of meaning is nearly gone. It is replaced with looking for opportunity to interject one's own chatter.

The chatter in today's world is evidence of a moral disease, treated only with mood altering medication.

A more effective remedy would be real speech. But speech can only come forth from the silence of the present moment, for it is in this eternal spot that truth resides. It is from here that beauty emanates, a self-revelation of the essence of being.

Speech requires the soul to open up, baring the goodness of its inner being. Other animals do not speak. They bark. They chirp. They snort. It is noise without reason. It is noise without self-revelation of inner being. A dog cannot express its moral goodness by panting, and it cannot express its moral corruption by growling. It is only capable of expressing instinctual responses to stimuli. It is the same with all animals, except the rational ones.

Chatter, however, is exactly what animals do, but without words. It is language deprived of meaning. Evil men, truly evil men, do not chatter. Think of the villain in a quiet room who speaks rarely and quietly but brings about great destruction with every word. He uses words to express only his moral depravity, often with a gentle and steady tone. But this is done with exactitude. It is done with focus. It is, in fact, closer in kind to morally righteous speech.

True speech is rare and powerful and beautiful. Chatter, on the other hand, is empty noise. It is empty of meaning. And it is horribly revealing of the empty self.

Reflection

- Do I use chatter as an outlet for nervous energy?
- How can I have deeper conversation with my loved ones?
- Am I afraid of prolonged silence?
- Consider how this verse applies to you: "Set a guard over my mouth, O Lord, / keep watch over the door of my lips!" (Psalms 141:3).

SILENCE IN WORDS[4]

Or

Where God Will Retire

A ssisi, Italy is a quiet place. It is built into the side of
a mountain. The stone roads are lined with stone
homes. The surrounding landscape is perfectly green. A
long-distance view shows no trace of the modern world.

---

[4]   Sister Marie-Aimée de Jésus (1839-1874) was a French Carmelite nun. She wrote the *Twelve Degrees of Silence* with St.
Benedict's *Twelve Degrees of Humility* in mind. Though Sr. Marie-Aimée wrote only a few lines or paragraphs on each of the
forms of silence, each is remarkably insightful. The real genius,
however, is in seeing silence in a holistic manner, applicable to
many areas of life. Her life and sanctity was known by her fellow
Carmelite St. Benedict of the Cross, also known as Edith Stein,
who was killed in the holocaust. It was customary for Carmel-
ites' biographies and writings to be shared with sister houses. It
is thus plausible that St. Thérèse of Lisieux read her works.

The *Twelve Degrees* build on each other, starting with the
obvious *Silence in Words*. I will consider only some of these
forms of silence. While I have been influenced by the *Twelve
Degrees*, the imperfection of the ideas should not be attributed
to Sr. Marie-Aimée.

Assisi today is not much different than the Assisi of 1181, the year St. Francis was born. I took my two oldest there, Aiden and Mary, fourteen and twelve respectively at the time.

We first spent a week in Rome seeing dead saints and beautiful basilicas. Inside, each church of Rome was like a sanctuary, an oasis from a chaotic world outside. I had to dodge city buses and mopeds and angry Italians. I had to watch my pockets as Gypsies followed me with sorrowful looks. Stepping into each church was like a conversion into the Church herself. I felt like I was stepping into the Arc of Salvation, escaping the floods of the sinful world.

Ah, but Assisi! The whole town is like a cathedral built by God. The countryside leading up the hill is like the nave. The stars overhead at night are like mosaics lining the ceiling. The medieval stone homes built by master craftsmen are like stained glass windows cut by master artists.

And then the tomb of St. Francis in the crypt of the basilica! This is like the sanctuary of God's cathedral— the cathedral that is Assisi. His body lays in a small gray box atop the tabernacle with the True Presence of Jesus Christ. Around the tomb and tabernacle rest Francis's first followers.

For me, Assisi is a sacred place like no other. There is something mystical about the town. There is something silent about the town. This silence is not due to people whispering or some community of silent monks. It is due to the Spirit of God. If God retired, He would do so in Assisi.

I believe I have always had a good relationship with my two oldest kids. Something deeper, however, occurred in Assisi. They felt a difference there. All three of us were content spending multiple hours a day praying at Francis's tomb. We walked up and down the mountain. We slowly toured the town. We ate plenty of gelato. But we always ended back in front of the tomb.

We were so joyful, and yet we said fewer words to each other than ever before. We, of course, spoke here and there but only with precise, interesting, and positive words. There was no complaining. There was no expression of desires for this or that. They were mostly words of insight or interest. Nothing was left unsaid. No one felt alone or ignored. It was perfect.

How I wished I could take a little of Assisi home with me! One way to brush up against Assisi, even from South Carolina, is to be actively aware of the present moment within the silence around us. I can choose, by my free will, to be present to my children, wrapped in silence. Fewer words can bring about greater presence. Fewer words can give silence the opportunity to make itself known. And it is in this great silence that God's presence can be felt, as we felt it in Assisi.

"The first indispensable step towards Divine union requires a practice of speaking less to the created and much to the Creator" (*The Twelve Degrees of Silence*, 40). When we converse with the Creator, we become more present to those around us.

We hear so many words, yet few resonate deeply within us. If everything is an alert, nothing is alarming, even when we see chaos all around. We have become desensitized to words, for the chatter never ceases. If it is not words bombarding us, it is some other form of noise that will not leave us alone. The present moment cannot be embraced while deciphering countless words.

Devices beeping and dinging, demanding attention, are usually backed with someone's words coming in through phone, email, social media, news flashes, texts. It is usually a distraction from the beauty and goodness in the present moment. What if I had spent the time in Assisi texting with my iPhone? The notion is like a clash of universes to me. I could have missed everything my kids and I experienced.

If we are flooded with words, how can we ever decipher important ones? Little children—who live only in the present—beg for mommy's attention, but mommy is trapped in a never-ceasing string of texts. She can hardly hear the only innocent voice in her life. Those words, coming from knee height, are worth listening to. Imagine Jesus letting the little children come to Him as they did in the Gospel. Now imagine Him staring at His smart phone and telling the kids to hold on a minute. Another clash of universes.

We are addicted to words coming at us, and we feel we

must respond in kind. The awkwardness of silence instantly moves people to speak. It was not so in past years. Men used to be happy sitting together on a front porch in silence. Now they have to stare at a little screen or share YouTube videos.

Modern man is terrified of a face staring at him across the table. Every quiet look feels like a death stare. "Say anything you want to me," the modern man's heart says, "just don't say nothing when you are with me." Such a man would not make it in Assisi.

Despite the never-ending stream of words coming at us, we must make a great effort to control our own words. The world will survive without our words.

Selectively choosing words takes extraordinary self-control. It is a task for a saint. "Set a guard over my mouth, O LORD, keep watch over the door of my lips!" (Ps 141:3).

For the extrovert, or, more precisely, the choleric or sanguine in temperament, sainthood may lie in mastering the urge to speak. It is easier to control a massive corporation than your own tongue. Why do we find the need to tell our own stories, to use our words to impress others, to sell ourselves under the guise of relationship building or finessing or even instilling confidence in the other? How much are we controlled by the simple inability to keep quiet? Assisi is a prescription. But there must be cheaper remedies. We can't all fly to Assisi for Morning Prayer.

God looks for little Assisi's around the world, cathedrals of His own making, silent places to take abode. Will my soul be such a place? Will I create an Assisi for Him?

Reflection

- Am I comfortable in silence with my friends and family?
- Do I use words to impress people or to escape boredom?
- Reflect on yesterday: how many words could I have cut and still have been just as productive?
- How does this passage speak to me? "But the Lord is in his holy temple; let all the earth keep silence before him" (Habakkuk 2:20).

Playing God

Or

Silence of the Imagination[5]

"But I say to you that every one who looks at a woman lustfully has already committed adultery with her in his heart." Matthew 5:28

The greatest inventions come from the use of imagination. There is no doubt of its value. We can close our eyes and imagine the first time we saw our true love. We can place ourselves in the story of the prodigal son and experience the Father's mercy. We can entertain children every night before bed with crazy stories of enchanted forests.

We can also, however, imagine a conversation with an enemy. We can role-play the martyr in our minds. We can sin at any moment with the power of imagination.

---

[5]   I am using the term *imagination* in the colloquial sense of drumming up a fictional account in our minds. This is to be distinguished from the scholastic or epistemological use of the term.

Imagination is our tool to live in the future, escaping the present moment. Silencing this aspect of imagination brings us back to the present, to reality. The future is fiction. It may never happen. The present takes no imagination. It takes perception. When the imagination runs on, we feel like gods in that we create other people's thoughts and words. We can write out the script of our friends, enemies, and our own heroic deeds. Usually, we caste ourselves as martyrs and others as villains. Whereas humility is the recognition of who we really are, imagination is an escape from who we really are. Often the person with the greatest imagination is the one with the greatest pride.

Of course, imagination is required to create works of art, music, literature. It is crucial to a wholesome life and wholesome society. It is crucial to leisure. Thank God for the imagination of Michelangelo and Vivaldi and Tolkien. If imagination is fueled by desire for truth and goodness, it can be even more real than the confines of this vale of tears in which we live.

But more often than not, imagination runs amuck as it searches for greener pastures on the other side of reality. It abandons the reality of today and seeks to homestead in the fiction of tomorrow. It abandons the people around us and replaces them with the people we wish them to be. And most of the time, we wish them to be something else because we are not willing to be something else ourselves. They must change because we will not.

Acceptance of those around us in the present moment

sharpens the mind to solve the day's problems. Imagination can then serve God the way it ought rather than taking His place as the creator of reality.

Reflection

- Do I allow my imagination to go too far?
- Do I demonize others and build myself up with imagination?
- Am I content with a quiet mind or must it stay on the go all the time?

THE DANGERS OF A GOOD MEMORY

Or

Silence of the Memory

"I will remember their sins and their misdeeds no more." Hebrews 10:17

"Then Peter came up and said to him, 'Lord, how often shall my brother sin against me, and I forgive him? As many as seven times?' Jesus said to him, 'I do not say to you seven times, but seventy times seven.'" Matthew 18:21–22

Memory is how we keep the past with us. It is necessary to have gratitude, to learn, to repent. Memory is a remarkable tool, like imagination.

It must be silenced at times. As we spoke of earlier, memory yields a nasty resentment. It brings back old feelings, creating a cesspool of anger and bitterness. It can cripple the subconscious. It can rationalize the disdain for people and cultures and activities that are not in themselves deserving of disdain. It can poison the mind.

Resentment is like drinking poison and waiting for the other person to die.

Memory is dangerous. It is unreliable. It can replay an event for its own purposes. It can vilify a person. It can canonize a person.

Memory has an iron grip. It can hold on to resentment to the point of rancor. And rancor rots the soul.

Worse yet, the iron grip can keep guilt alive far longer than it ought. It morphs the guilt into self-pity, turning humility into a left-handed pride. Self-pity can be devastating to all around you, especially those who depend on your success.

Memory is the springboard for all these ailments of the mind. By silencing the memory, we can consider people, places, and things in themselves without resentment, bitterness, prejudice, envy, or nostalgia.

How many virtues have been stonewalled by infected memories of pain and discord? Allow the past to be the past and the present to be the present.

Reflection

- Do I hold grudges?
- Do I make a point of forgiving people . . . over and over again?
- Who in my life needs forgiveness continuous- ly and why?

THE NEGATIVE OF TOO MUCH POSITIVE

Or

Silence of the Heart

"He who loves pleasure will be a poor man." Proverbs 21:17

One of my greatest joys is to watch the children play together, especially when the bigger kids play with the little kids. They feed off each other. One kid laughs and causes the other to laugh harder. Then they begin doing something goofy like climbing all over each other or jumping on the couch and landing on each other. One of them has that experience of "this is funny" but it brushes right up to the margin of "this is painful." It's like when the little kids asked to be tickled. They want that tickle to barely cross the threshold of pain, but not too far.

As I watch the kids getting rougher and rougher and laughing louder and louder, I can almost see an invisible red line between fun and anger. Astoundingly, they don't see it. Not even the teenagers. Everyone is just pushing the fun an inch further. Then . . . *boom!* That red line is crossed, someone is hurt. They get furious. One of them is in tears. The other gets defensive. Sometimes the one hurt throws a real punch. Total war ensues.

This happens in my house frequently—as in every day. It is a difficult thing to guard against. It is a difficult thing to teach the bigger kids to avoid. It is difficult because eighty percent of it was good and wholesome. Eighty percent should be encouraged. That laughter, that playing, a little roughhousing, it's what I live for as a parent. It's what will forge memories of a joyful household.

It is like so many of our passions or emotions in life. It is not the passions themselves that get us into trouble, but rather their excess.

Throughout all of intellectual history, philosophers have struggled over the value of emotions. In the Greek tradition alone, there is a school of thought for nearly every approach to them: Stoics suppress them all; Epicureans seek pleasure; and Aristotelians seek to harmonize their reason and passions. The passions may be essential for self-preservation, but they are also our greatest enemy if left unguarded. It was Buddha who said, "A man who conquers himself is greater than one who conquers a thousand men in battle."

If a man has looked around, he can see the dire need for human beings to silence the passions on occasion.

It may seem obvious to silence negative or harmful feelings. But the monastic tradition has found deeper reasons that are not so obvious. Even the many positive feelings we have toward people and things and places we love require purification. My kids should probably refrain from the positive emotions at times. We should, as a family, embrace a little stoicism to purge ourselves of that excitement and busyness and energy that occupies our heart. Often that positive energy comes from just being hyper. As a father, I must find ways to help them express joy on a deeper level than just body slamming each other.

The heart is so important, but it must be purged on occasion, like getting an oil change in the car. A better analogy might be the human heart itself. The devil uses our purest desires and healthy attachments as slow producers of plaque to build up blockage against the love of God. God requires seamless, unencumbered flow through our heart. This is why saintly people detach from worldly affairs, even honorable ones. This is why cloistered nuns detach even from their loving family—a truly unique calling. This is why the desert fathers looked out over barrenness rather than the beautiful walls of a cathedral. It is said that St. Alphonsus Liguori diverted his eyes from the beautiful artwork in the churches of Rome because he wanted only God to reside in his soul. This might be extreme for me and my family, but there is a lesson to be learned.

Our hearts need purifying so that they rest in God

alone. Not just St. Augustine's heart. Not just St. Alphonsus's heart. Not just my heart. But the same must be said about the hearts of all twelve of my children. How to do this in a joyful, loud, rambunctious family is a mystery like the Holy Trinity itself. But that doesn't mean I'll stop trying to figure it out.

Reflection

- Do I think the ascetic desert fathers were crazy or just crazy in love with God?
- Why would God want me to "silence" positive emotions on occasion?
- Do I rely too much on "good feelings" about God and family?

Playing Poorly With a Stacked Deck

Or

Silence of Self-love

*"Whoever would save his life will lose it, and who-
ever loses his life for my sake will find it." Matthew
16:25*

Two young nuns were walking through a cloistered
convent. The first nun dropped a pitcher of water
and it shattered on the ground. She left to get a broom,
and the second nun waited there so no one would step
on the glass. The Mother Superior happened to walk
through the room and saw the young nun standing next
to the shattered glass. She gave her three Hail Marys
as a penance for being clumsy and dropping the pitcher. Immediately, the young nun explained that she was
just guarding the shards of glass for the other sister who
dropped the pitcher. Then the Mother Superior gave her

ten more Hail Marys for being unwilling to take on such a small penance for her sister.

How often are we fixated on defending ourselves? How often do we need to think others are inferior to us? *They are not leaders like us. They do not work hard like us. They are not as giving as us. They do not understand us.* This is nothing but the need to defend ourselves to ourselves. Even if one has mastered the tongue, he may still defend himself to himself. Thus, silencing the tongue is just the beginning. We must silence our own self-love.

If I know how much criticism I deserve, if I know that any little accomplishment I have is due to the grace of God, if I know He could have easily given the blessing, the work ethic, or the opportunities to another, I will then realize that I should only be criticizing myself in my mind, not anyone else.

Another person should only come to mind while praying for them or admiring them. Yes, there are those who I find annoying or lazy or immoral. They may be. But they may have done far more with the gifts given to them than I have with those given to me. They may be playing cards very well with half a deck, and I may be playing poorly with an entire deck that is stacked in my favor! If I constantly remember this, self-love would be supplanted with admiration for others.

When self-love has been silenced, I embrace the present moment. I meet my real self. And then my real self encounters others. It is like coming eye to eye with someone after standing on a tall podium and looking down on them. The other could be seven feet tall, but since you were twenty feet high, you never noticed. Silencing self-love enables me to meet people for the first time.

Silencing self-love allows room for the presence of God to reside within. And then this presence within me unites with the presence of God in others.

Reflection

- Read the following verse quickly. Then read it slowly. Then read it a third time very slowly. Consider how God is speaking to you. "Then Jesus said to his disciples, 'If any man would come after me, let him deny himself and take up his cross and follow me. For whoever would save his life will lose it, and whoever loses his life for my sake will find it. For what will it profit a man, if he gains the whole world and forfeits his life?" (Matthew 16:24–26).

- How many ways can I decrease self-love?

GOD AIN'T IN NO IVORY TOWER

Or

Silence of the Intellect

"Every one who is arrogant is an abomination to the Lord; be assured, he will not go unpunished." Proverbs 16:5

I seem to have too many friends with higher education. One such friend, a professor at a university in Europe who speaks numerous languages and has numerous advanced degrees, met me for lunch one day. The nicest place in this small midwestern town was a cheap Italian restaurant chain.

Our waitress was a good midwestern girl who probably worked a breakfast shift at the diner down the road. I bet she had never even left the state in her life.

"Hey guys," she said, cheerfully introducing herself. She took our drink order, came back a few minutes later, and said, "Ready to order?" "Yes ma'am," I said. "OK, what can I get you?" she asked. I ordered my meal.

"How 'bout you?" she said turning to my friend with a big smile.

What he did made me want to crawl under the table and hide. He rattled off the rather long name of the dish in the thickest Italian accent he could muster, as if he was sitting in the finest café in Milan. I couldn't understand a word he said. The waitress said, "What was that?" I could have died. He repeated the order exactly the same way.

"Honey, you're gonna have to slow down." So he did. He pedantically said his order really slow, pronouncing each syllable like he was talking to a child. "Oh, I gotcha. Alrighty. I'll get that right in." She walked away. I was stuck there at the table with a *prima donna*.

Conversation with this person was always interesting. But I was scandalized. The atmosphere at my table was now so filthy that I wanted to douse myself in hand sanitizer.

Education has a purpose. It is not to show up waitresses in cheap Italian restaurants.

Shakespeare said knowledge maketh a bloody entry, meaning truth is difficult to learn and we must pay a cost to obtain it. This is fully true. But the axiom can be used another way in our context. Knowledge can make a bloody entry as self-inflicted spiritual wounds. So much pride comes with knowledge, especially book knowledge. It is an easy way to classify ourselves as beyond other simpletons. It is a way to pretend we are more refined.

Nothing turns God away more than thinking we can

reach Him with our intellect. How many Catholic intellectuals have built their very own Tower of Babel! And they try to live on the top floor of this tower, separating themselves from the common man below.

Father Michael Scanlon, of happy memory, once said that God rejects the proud even when they are right.

We must silence our intellect, recognizing that faith is the true path to understanding God. *Fides quarens intellectum* is a Latin phrased used by St. Anselm meaning "faith seeking understanding." In other words, faith—not brains—brings understanding of God. You cannot develop a personal relationship with God by merely filling your mind with education.

How is it that cloistered nuns can be dubbed Doctors of the Church? Their insight was not found by reading dissertations but in finding the real presence of God in their daily activities. God is found in taking out the trash, sweeping the floor, tending to the sick, and changing diapers. God is found there. Books should help us set the context of this work, to reinforce the rationality of virtuous living, to study the thoughts of holy men and woman that came before us. But we must spend time with someone to get to know them personally.

If we stay with God long enough in prayer and holy works, we begin to learn His nature, His attributes, His language, His goals for us. This is real theology. This is the study of God at the most granular level. God is not living up in the ivory tower. He is at the fishing docks preaching the kingdom of God. He is healing lepers, the lame, the blind. He is with the children. If we are looking for Him, where shall we go? I would guess He is not in the finest café in Milan. My friend is no longer at the finest café either. He is now a broken man, alone, with only his education to keep him company.

Reflection

- Do I take pride (even a little) in my IQ, my education, or my experience?
- How is Jesus speaking to me in the following parable from Luke 18:9–14? "He also told this parable to some who trusted in themselves that they were righteous and despised others: 'Two men went up into the temple to pray, one a Pharisee and the other a tax collector. The Pharisee stood and prayed thus with himself, "God, I thank you that I am not like other men, extortioners, unjust, adulterers, or even like this tax collector. I fast twice a week, I give tithes of all that I get." But the tax collector, standing far off, would not even lift up his eyes to heaven, but beat his breast, saying, "God, be merciful to me a sinner!" I tell you, this man went down to his house justified rather than the other; for every one who exalts himself will be humbled, but he who humbles himself will be exalted.'"

PART THREE
STILLNESS

Introduction to Stillness

Or

Finding Stillness Amidst the Storm

"And a great storm of wind arose, and the waves beat into the boat, so that the boat was already filling. But he was in the stern, asleep on the cushion; and they woke him and said to him, 'Teacher, do you not care if we perish?' And he awoke and rebuked the wind, and said to the sea, 'Peace! Be still!' And the wind ceased, and there was a great calm. He said to them, 'Why are you afraid? Have you no faith?' And they were filled with awe, and said to one another, 'Who then is this, that even wind and sea obey him?'"
Mark 4:37–41

The boat began to rock faster and faster. The swaying turned from a gentle up and down to violent jolts, knocking them off their feet. A few apostles almost fell overboard. The movement was just too much.

As the winds blew faster, so did their breath. They were

exhausted from fighting the storm. There was no relief in sight. The storm moved faster still. The waves grew larger still. The speed of everything was terrifying.

And Jesus slept.

Watching Jesus sleep added to the stress of the storm. The apostles not only had to battle Mother Nature but they had to do so themselves; Jesus wouldn't even lend a helping hand—or so they thought.

And so we think.

How often we feel that Jesus is sleeping while life's storm grows faster. With speed comes violence. With too much movement comes sickness. Life is like those brutal winds that rise to the level of a vortex, tossing us to and fro. Our job, our family, our sufferings; does it ever slow down? How can life get any faster without our boat turning over, leaving us to drown in the sea of despair?

Why is Jesus sleeping while our storm rages on?

But not a moment too soon, Jesus—the Lord of lords and King of kings—extended His almighty hand and raised His almighty voice, "Peace. Be still." And all of the earth's natural powers obeyed Him. The earth bowed down to its Creator. The wind folded up as angels' wings do when they bow before His heavenly throne. The waters calmed so still and smooth, like a royal carpet rolled out for His feet to walk upon.

"And there was a great calm."

The apostles were filled with awe at this man who even the winds and sea obey. We too must be filled with awe.

But we need not ask, "Who then is this, that even wind and sea obey Him?" The apostles had not yet received the full revelation. But the winds and waters knew, and we must be like them. Yes, we know who holds our lives in the palm of His hand, who grips us tightly as Peter's hand gripped the line. Jesus will never let us go.

In this life, we will surely encounter trial and tribulation. But Jesus offers us peace—not just in the next life but in this one too. Yes, if we can hear His command amidst the storms of life to have peace and to be still, then we will be on our way to become a saint in heaven with Him forever. Part three of this book attempts to explain how to do just that.

The Devil's Trojan Horse

Or

The Sin of Sloth

When I used to think of sloth, I thought of a couch potato, laying around, disgusting and exhausted. In the end, I was right, but for all the wrong reasons.

I hadn't been on a spiritual retreat in fifteen years. Dr. Bob Schuchts, the retreat master, invited me to one on the topic of suffering and healing. The subject was related to a project at work and Dr. Bob offered it to me for free. I was looking to study the subject of suffering and healing, not to study myself. I was in for a surprise.

Dr. Bob explained that in order for healing to occur, we must first isolate our root deadly sin and diagnose why it is so. Laying beneath this root sin may be wounds that we never fully recognized.

I enjoyed the challenge. I had read enough spiritual works to know that a personal inventory of the seven deadly sins is often the first step to spiritual advancement.

So I threw myself into the retreat and trusted something good would come out of it.

I was shocked. At the beginning of the retreat, I would have said that the sin of sloth was the least of my problems. I work hard. I work out hard. I don't watch too much TV. I'm always moving, especially with the kids. People say to me, "How do you do it all?" I'm the farthest person from sloth, right? Plus, I'm a guy with a temper. Anger and sloth felt like opposites to me. Anger gets your engine running. Sloth puts on the brakes. These two sins can't exist in me at the same time, right?

Wrong.

By the end of the retreat, I thought something very different.

I did not understand that my fast-paced lifestyle was a feeding ground for sloth. It is exactly what the devil wants of big engine people. He wants me to rev my engine and go into a tail spin. He wants me to hear the engine reaching top RPMs. He wants me to see the dust flying up around me. He wants me to feel like I'm getting somewhere, and fast. All the while, I am going nowhere, like a hamster on a wheel.

I am not unique. Many people suffer from this deceptive sin without knowing it. It is similar to someone with an autoimmune disease, like Lupus, who continually treats the newest ailment without ever knowing why they got it so easily. Sloth is hard to diagnose in part because we stay busy dealing with envy or gluttony or lust or anger or pride. Certainly pride is the root of all sin. It is also hard to see in ourselves. But there is a lot of focus on pride. Priests talk about it from the pulpit. Leadership books talk about servant leadership. People don't like arrogance. Most would admit that humility is crucial to success and happiness.

With sloth, however, people are confused. No one talks about it—ever. It is the forgotten vice. They don't see it. They don't know how to remedy it. Thus, the devil sees an opening, especially in the modern world.

Sun Tzu said, "All warfare is based on deception. Hence, when we are able to attack, we must seem unable; when using our forces, we must appear inactive." There is perhaps no more deceptive sin than sloth. It is the devil's weapon of choice in today's world. Sloth is the devil's Trojan horse that brings the rest of the deadly sins into our frantically busy, modern American lifestyle.

Modern Americans are plagued by a deceptively dangerous form of sickness: the inability to be still. The reason for this is the sin of sloth. That may be counterintuitive. Again, when I used to think of sloth, I thought of a couch potato, laying around, disgusting and exhausted. This is probably the common image that comes to most minds. While this may be one manifestation of sloth, it is not the only one. It is certainly not the devil's favorite form of sloth.

Those who feel too busy to pray, too cash-strapped to tithe, too frantic to enjoy God's many blessings—

especially the present moment—may be a victim of the devil's silent killer.

The devil has chosen this capital sin for the modern world precisely because of the busyness, chaos, flashing lights and noisy airways, ringing iPhones, fast food, multi-tasking, social media, and all those features of modern life. Consider the business executive buying another time management book or the soccer mom overwhelmed with her kid's school and sports schedule: they have filled not only their calendar with too many events but their hearts with anxiety. The modern man and woman would never consider themselves lazy. How could one who is constantly moving be lazy? This is why most people do not confess the sin of sloth, whether to a priest or to themselves.

Sloth is not laziness *per se*. It is not anything *per se*, which is the difficulty in defining it. The other capital sins—pride, envy, gluttony, lust, anger, greed—are active. They are sins of commission. Sloth is inactive. It is a sin of omission.

Thomas Aquinas defines sloth as "sorrow for spiritual goods" and "sluggishness of the mind which neglects to begin good" (II-II, Q. 35, Art. 1). "Sorrow" does not seem applicable to the hustle and bustle of the modern world with its millions of advertisements and selfie pictures. Neither does "sluggishness" seem apropos amidst the fastest moving culture in world history. And yet depression and exhaustion are rampant. The attributes of modern life are fostering the sin of sloth to an unparalleled extent. We must look at the cesspool of busyness and see how it incubates a "sorrow for spiritual goods."

The kid's travel soccer team has a tournament on Sunday. Do we still go to Mass? Sloth says that we are too busy for Mass. We shrug our shoulders and say somewhat sadly, "I can't do everything. I'm sure God understands." Sloth sees Morning Prayer as asking too much. "I need my coffee to start my day. God wants me to just chill out. I need my own time right now." Sloth sees a family Rosary at night as a bit extreme. "We are good people. And by night, we are exhausted because of our hard work all day. It is awkward to pray together anyway. It is better to have family fun watching that new comedy on TV." Sloth tells us that liturgy must be cool and entertaining and that tradition and classical beauty is outdated and ineffective. "Why can't Mass be fun, especially for the kids!"

Sloth puts God in a little box that fits nicely and neatly into the complex design of our lives. We designate time and place for God. Sloth forgets that all other activities—business meetings, soccer games, food, sex, golf, social work—are all means to making us holier before God. Every activity in life, from our own conception to natural death, is for the purpose of getting us to heaven. In short, sloth tells us, "No, this is too extreme! God doesn't ask everyone to be like those crazy saints. Work-life balance is the key."

We must take our own moral inventory and see how

much clutter is taking up the finite space of our hearts—all of which belongs to God.

The irony of the whole thing is that the most productive people in history have been saints. Holiness provides a great rule of life. When one begins each day with prayer, especially daily Mass, the rest of the day seems to fall into place. When one begins a business meeting with a quick internal prayer, the focus and attention is much greater. When one prays a family Rosary at night, the days seems to wind down with a peaceful finish. When the entire week is built around Sunday Mass as a family, it makes the many other decisions much easier to resolve.

This has been my experience, and yet sloth continues to attack me. I can feel at times the desire for goodness being drained from me, like I have a leak in my soul. If I don't plug the leak with prayer and fasting and tithing and corporal works of mercy, I become an empty shell.

If we had spiritual X-ray vision and could see the soul, I don't think we would see the folks on TV and the folks running around big cities and yuppie communities as the perfect people they display. I think we would see something more akin to the walking dead. I think we would see a fast-moving shell that has been drained of desire for spiritual goods.

What would we see if we looked at ourselves?

Would we see couch potato souls, laying around, disgusting and exhausted? Would we see the empty shells with no desire for the things of God?

In a way, I was right about the image of sloth, but it applies to the soul more than the body.

Reflection

- How does sloth manifest in my life?
- Do I get engaged, excited, and passionate about spiritual goods or just temporal goods?
- Do I save energy for God or do I burn out on worldly pursuits?

PACING BEHIND HOME PLATE

Or

Abandon the Obsession With Progress

"Be still, and know that I am God." Psalms 46:10

I was running with a buddy. We ended up talking about kids, as usual. He was telling me how rigorous his daughter's schedule was for soccer: travel teams with overnight trips, speed and agility training at high end facilities, overnight summer camps with expert coaches. "Wow," I thought to myself. "She must be college scholarship material." But I was confused because I thought his daughter was rather young. I must be mistaken. "How old is your daughter?" I asked. "She's ten."

This dad is not doing anything out of the ordinary in today's world. In fact, I remember when my first kid started playing sports at six or seven and how serious I took it. I looked at each of his moves, judging his athletic ability. He quickly became focused as a baseball catcher. I would pace back and forth behind home plate, judging

121

every move he made, talking to him throughout the game. I did not know how utterly obnoxious I was. Now I see a dad doing this in my younger kids' leagues and I think, "What an idiot. Sit down, dad. You ain't helping."

Why did I do this? Because I was only concerned about the progress he would make. I did not enjoy the game enough. I did not enjoy watching him enough. Certainly there is a time and place to "make progress." There is a time and place to plan for the future. But behind home plate during a game is not it.

Having numerous kids is a good remedy to this obsession with progress. While I still want my kids to achieve excellence in certain areas of life, and I want them to excel at whatever they commit to, I am much better now at sitting still, watching the game, and enjoying the present moment.

Sitting still. No more pacing back and forth behind home plate. Enjoy the game. Why is this so hard? Why is this so hard in sports, at home, even at work? Why does everyone have to be on the go?

Calvin Coolidge said, "Don't you know that four fifths of all our troubles in this life would disappear if we would just sit down and keep still?"

He was correct.

There is a reason man is tempted to move. All created things in the universe, Aristotle says, are moving. He found that movement can only be caused by movement, and thus a Prime Mover, that which moves but is unmoved, necessarily exists. It is natural to want to move, for we have been moving since the moment of our conception.

Modern man is obsessed with movement because he is obsessed with progress. This obsession thrusts man—especially parents—into constant action. Movement, any movement, is considered productive. The modern man is like a child with attention deficit disorder unable to sit still. He would rather walk in a circle than sit in silence. This is why kids don't have time to breathe. They go from school to sports to homework to more sports to music lessons to therapy and back to more homework. It is as if the modern parent wants a bunch of gerbils for children, running on the wheel. Gerbils are more fun to watch when they are moving.

To overcome the anxiety that is sweeping through our schools like the bubonic plague, we must learn to sit still. This does not mean boring kids. This doesn't mean loser kids. It doesn't mean we are lazy parents. It does mean, however, that movement for the sake of movement is a tool of the devil. It is more commonly said that idleness is the tool of the devil. But stillness is not idleness.

Herein lies a crucial distinction.

Idleness lacks purpose. Shopping for no purpose, or watching TV for no purpose, or eating for no purpose is idleness. Even lifting weights for no purpose is idleness. True stillness—a stillness wrapped in silence—is rigorous focus on one thing. And the fruits of this focus can be life-changing.

Ever since the Enlightenment, the present moment has been seen as insufficient. Every present moment has been sacrificed on the altar of progress. Progress is always down the road. You must travel to get there. Being still, it is believed, will never achieve progress. And yet you can never satisfy its ruthless calling. It calls even after you have dropped in exhaustion. It calls you like the Sirens that poisoned the ears of Odysseus, turning him into a madman willing to jump ship and drown trying to reach them.

Progress is inexhaustible in the sense that you will never attain the goal. The present moment, however, is likewise inexhaustible but in the sense that it can be embraced for eternity without boredom or stiffness or jealousy of others or distraction from the past and future. You cannot embrace the present moment if you are moving for the sake of moving. That is why we must learn to sit still.

There is more healing found in the present moment, in silence, in stillness than in all the usefulness for sale by commercialism and all the innovation found in progress. My family and I can be made whole again in the present. Commercialism and progress simply show us what we are not. It is a path to regret and anxiety.

My kids are not gerbils. They are made in the image and likeness of God, and they must identify with this image and likeness. They do not become more like this image and likeness by doing lots and lots of stuff. They find their true identity by coming in contact with God who is found in the present moment, in silence, in stillness.

No more pacing behind home plate. Sit down and enjoy the game.

Reflection

- Do I feel a need to keep moving unnecessarily?
- Do I focus too much on progress—for myself, my spouse, my kids—rather than virtue?
- In what ways is God asking me to speed up, and in what ways is He asking me to slow down?
- Say the following passage seven times slowly in prayer: "Be still, and know that I am God" (Psalms 46:10).

THE ENEMY OF
CORPORATE AMERICA

Or

Be Content With What You Have.
It Feels Better Anyway.

"'Peace! Be still!' And the wind ceased, and there was a great calm." Mark 4:39

My dad has published values-oriented books for children for most of my life. Now, I am part of the fourth generation in the same family business. I remember my mom using one of his books to help me learn to read. There was a story about a monkey who reached his hand into a hole in a tree in order to grab some acorns lying inside it. But his closed fist would not fit back through the hole. He was trapped. In order to remove his hand, he had to let go of his prize.

It is funny what images and stories stick in your mind. More than thirty years later, I can see in my mind's eye the picture of that monkey with his closed fist stuck in that tree.

Raising kids in a consumeristic society reminds me of this monkey. I see the kids get their eyes fixed on something, like getting a new computer. They can't let go of it. They can't get their mind off of it. And they get stuck like that monkey's fist in the hole.

Consumerism calls to us through advertisements, peer pressure, and the never-ending promise of greater pleasure tomorrow than we have today. One reason we spend so much money today is that we are uncomfortable being still in our own house. As Blaise Pascal famously said, "All of humanity's problems stem from man's inability to sit quietly in a room alone." As soon as stir-crazy sets in and people load up in the car, you can bet your life that money will be spent. "Well, we needed to get this anyway," makes it all OK.

Worse yet, we are uncomfortable in our own skin. It is as if we can buy our way out of ourselves. Consumerism tells us, especially children, how much more fun they can have, how much cooler they can be, if they just got this one thing. It really has nothing to do with the product. The features are never pushed, only the benefits to your life. Marketers figured this out, but consumers have not.

I notice advertisements much more now that I am a dad. I went into an Abercrombie and Fitch store a few years back looking at a clearance rack for my teenagers (my wife would have known better). I was surrounded by teenagers. Teenagers shopping, teenagers working, a teenager walking around spraying cologne or perfume throughout the store, and teenagers wrapped around the wall in advertisements.

One huge picture caught my attention. It was of a teenage boy. He must have been twenty feet long. He lined the entire wall. He was laying on his side, resting on his elbow, giving the really laid-back feel. The picture was from the waist up. Then I realized he had no shirt on. Then I looked around the rest of the walls and advertisements. Most of the pictures had teenagers with almost no clothes on. Maybe swimsuits. Maybe headshots from the neck up. But there were absolutely no clothes being advertised. How could this be given that I was in a clothing store? I got an eerie feeling. I got an evil feeling. They were not selling clothes to teenagers. They were selling seductiveness. I think the executives of this company and those like them will have serious questions to answer on Judgment Day. "And he said to his disciples, 'Temptations to sin are sure to come; but woe to him by whom they come! It would be better for him if a millstone were hung round his neck and he were cast into the sea, than that he should cause one of these little ones to sin'" (Lk 17:1–2).

As parents, we, too, must not lead our little ones astray by raising them as part of this culture. If they live a shopping mall lifestyle, they will learn to desire the Abercrombie and Fitch lifestyle. The consumerism is just too much for them to withstand.

Rather, we must teach them to be content with what they have, to buy things only when necessary, and to use money to meet a true need rather than a silly fantasy. One of the surest ways to resist the temptations spewed out by consumerism is stillness.

Stillness doesn't cost anything. Enjoying the family's company on Saturday doesn't cost anything. Finding joy in simple things—hiking, reading, drawing, playing an instrument—costs very little. How content can we be without succumbing to the calls of consumerism?

But there is an even greater danger now. Consumerism used to call us to get up and move. Now we can be called to remain on the couch and click "download" and "stream" and "same day delivery." We can be sucked into consumerism without leaving the house. But this is still movement. It is a psychological reach into the hole to grab something. It is even more seductive than the need to drive somewhere. It feels so seamless, so effortless. It feels less chaotic. It provides an artificial sense of stillness or serenity. It is, however, just that: artificial.

Stillness is not a mere lack of physical motion any more than silence is a mere lack of sound. Stillness is rather a spiritual peace, a serenity in the present moment. Just as silence wraps around a beautiful song, stillness can be present within a person moving.

I think of Ghandi. He walked hundreds of miles in silent protest of the racism in India. Countless people followed him. I envision him walking at a brisk pace along dirt roads, waving and smiling at the poor and oppressed. I see him ruffling the hair of the small children walking beside him. He was moving, but there was a great stillness within him. Ghandi wasn't searching to quench a thirst for pleasure. He had a great stillness within. He even said one time, "I do not live to eat. I eat to live." This is interior stillness. This is what we want our children to have.

I compare this to the Black Lives Matter movement, the protests, the riots, the raiding of shops and breaking of windows and burning of police cars. Here, I see anger and envy. I see immaturity and stupidity. I see external chaos, of course. But I also see internal chaos, a spiritual emptiness. Here, there is no internal stillness. There is anxiety. But this behavior did not spring from nowhere. It sprang from a culture obsessed with violence, self-indulgence, a sense of entitlement, a demand for instant gratification. These protestors have nothing in common with Ghandi. He would be ashamed, as would Martin Luther King, Jr., of these barbaric protestors. When I see these protestors, I see the victory of consumerism: an internal restlessness resulting in explosions of violence.

If a customer is still, if a customer is content in the present moment, he is a tough sale. Ghandi was a terrible customer. Anybody with great interior stillness is a terrible customer. Thus, Corporate America needs to remind consumers just how bored they really are. Corporate America needs anxious customers who need to satiate that urge to consume, whether eternally or internally.

Stillness is the enemy of Corporate America.

Stillness will never reach into the hole to grab the acorns. And without the reach, the world will never trap us.

Reflection

- Do I shop out of boredom?
- Do I get cabin fever or stir crazy too easily?
- Read this passage quickly. Then read it slowly. Read it a third time really slowly: "But he was in the stern, asleep on the cushion; and they woke him and said to him, 'Teacher, do you not care if we perish?' And he awoke and rebuked the wind, and said to the sea, 'Peace! Be still!' And the wind ceased, and there was a great calm" (Mark 4:38–39).

MAKING PEOPLE OUT OF CLAY

Or

The Dangers of Curiosity

"Him who slanders his neighbor secretly I will destroy. The man of haughty looks and arrogant heart I will not endure." Psalms 101:5

I consider myself a very curious person. I have lots of interests. I can talk with anyone so long as they are sincere. I have read books on every subject from punctuation to the mathematical theory of infinite. The internet would seem to be my best friend, but it is actually my worst enemy. It allows me to jump from one topic to the next, allowing my active mind to skim across subjects like a smooth stone over water. This may sound great to an active mind. But in reality, it inhibits deep thinking.

Wikipedia, for example, is extremely convenient. But I have never once gotten through a single entry before clicking a link to another subject. The other day I started on the Korean War, and ten minutes later I was on

Rasputin. I learned almost nothing. It was like watching the History Channel commercials rather than a History Channel documentary.

What if we tried to educate our kids by having them read one random page at a time out of every book on the shelf? They would learn stuff, but their minds would not learn the discipline of deep work, which is infinitely more valuable than stuff. They would develop some version of attention deficit disorder.

Curiosity is a gift to human nature. It has led to many great discoveries and innovations. *Undisciplined* curiosity, however, yanks a person from the present moment and thrusts them headlong into unnecessary motion. Education requires stillness, a stillness of body, a stillness of mind.

With our never-ceasing feed of social media, e-mail, notifications beeping and dinging on our phones, we have become curious about everything from the president's latest tweet to Hollywood's latest divorce. And yet, for all the time in front of a screen, we learn very little.

Undisciplined curiosity pushes us into the past and future. It wonders what the real story was behind the dramatic dispute between two people. It wonders what will happen when a series of events changes our situation. It wonders what other people think about us. It takes away the internal stillness required for peace of mind. It only leads to anxiety, and Christ warns us about being anxious about tomorrow.

As my kids grew into middle school and high school, I noticed their conversations began to change. I would hear them talking about other kids. They would recount what one kid said to another. They would speculate as to what the real story was behind a dispute. They would guess whether this girl would accept this guy's invitation to a dance. It rubbed me the wrong way—big time.

While this can begin as harmless fun, it forms a very bad habit. It can become meddlesome. It can become gossip or even slander. At one point, I put my foot down and said, "No more!" It is simply not acceptable. Allowing curiosity to bubble up is an occasion of sin.

It may sound radical, but the only legitimate interest in other people's affairs is searching for a way to help them. Period. Any other curiosity, any other movement into their zone of privacy, is trespassing.

When I think or speak of someone, I try to imagine being in their house as a guest. If they leave the room, would I begin rummaging through desk draws or bedrooms? I wouldn't dare. Most people wouldn't dare. At most, I would look at the spines of books on a shelf, but only in the room they left me. Why then would I be willing to rummage through their reputation or private matters? I must approach others, even in my own mind, with a spirit of stillness like I would sit quietly on their couch waiting for them to return.

Curiosity of the mind is not the only problem. Obviously, curiosity of the eyes is a terrible disturber of our interior stillness. Many temptations and impure images enter the soul through the eyes. They become part of you. In a way, they can never be erased. But I'm not even talking about that here. I'm talking about a much subtler danger that comes from curiosity of the eyes: the judgments we make about people simply by seeing them.

Curiosity of the eyes thrusts our soul into useless motion. How often do we people watch and pass tiny judgments on people's dress, their shoes, their overall polish? How often do we think we can sum up a person in seconds? We are good people readers, we tell ourselves. And yet we fail to read the man in the mirror. In reading people we should consider the eyes as our potential enemy. At the same time, I have found my gut reaction to someone is usually proven right. This does not mean, however, that it was right to even have a gut reaction. The person deserves more than my gut. They deserve my attention, my listening, my presumption that they are good and honorable. Any other snap judgment is like balling up my pride and throwing it right in their face. "Here! That's what you are!"

As sound must be wrapped in silence, so must curiosity be wrapped in stillness.

If we cultivate and possess interior stillness, it will serve as the clay upon which we allow others to imprint themselves, their whole selves, rather than a mold into which we will cast them based on superficial interactions.

I don't make people out of clay. God does.

Reflection

- How often do I talk about people's shortcomings behind their back?
- Do I pretend the gossip is for good reason?
- Read the following passage from King David and consider why God sees curiosity into other people's affairs as so insidious: "Him who slanders his neighbor secretly I will destroy. The man of haughty looks and arrogant heart I will not endure" (Psalms 101:5).

Waiting for the Airport Shuttle

Or

Every Moment Is a Moment to Be Still

"And after the earthquake a fire, but the Lord *was not in the fire; and after the fire a still small voice."*
1 Kings 19:12

It was 10:00 p.m. My flight from Chicago had just landed. I was forced to check my carry-on because airlines cram people in like sardines. After leaving the baggage claim, I stepped out into the Charlotte humidity that felt like the Amazon jungle. I walked toward the daily parking shuttle bus location. And I waited. More people came to wait. And we kept waiting and waiting. Everyone around me began to complain. Where the hell is the bus? Doesn't anyone know how to run a transportation system? It's so stinking hot out here! My blood began to boil like everyone else's.

Around the twenty-minute mark, I realized the irony of the situation. I had just finished writing a section of this book on the plane about stillness. And I laughed to myself. What a hypocrite you are, Conor!

So I stood there, holding my roller bag with fifty people around me, all sweating and some complaining. I decided to be still. I did not stand any differently. I did not sit like a Buddhist monk. I just calmed down.

I called to mind that God is found in the present moment. He is right there with me as I wait for the bus. I did not have to go somewhere to find Him. I did not have to be surrounded by religious articles. I did not have to escape the world. I just had to, for a minute, not be of the world.

I called to mind that I could embrace a little bit of silence even though noise surrounded me—cars and buses, whistles blowing and horns honking, frustrated people, airplanes in the distance. If I listened, I could hear a gentle silence that survived the clashing of noises. It sounded beautiful.

I called to my mind the stillness that I could enjoy right there. I relaxed my body and instantly felt my shoulders and back and neck loosen. It felt good. It almost felt like flopping down on the couch after a long day.

More importantly, I found an interior stillness. I'm positive my heartbeat slowed, and I wasn't even thinking about that. I intentionally calmed all the movement going on in my mind. It was like my brain slowed down.

I focused on finding God in that stillness and nothing else. I closed my eyes for just a few seconds, and then I felt something. I felt a cool breeze. It was partly from the tunnel-like structure I was standing in. It was partly from buses flying by. I felt it all over my body. My mind took me to Hilton Head beach, standing on the shore with the cool breeze blowing in from the Atlantic. I opened my eyes, so relaxed, so at peace. The people and buses seemed to move slower, like I was in a slow-motion movie.

There is a tremendous difference between emptying the mind and focusing the mind. Eastern religion and philosophy, both of which have invaded Western civilization, support the notion of "emptying oneself." A dangerous notion. Our souls are not made to be empty. Something will fill it up. If we do not have the presence of God within us, the presence of evil spirits will take His place.

We rational creatures have an intellect and will. We are engineered by God to focus on things. The trick—if I can call it that—is to focus on one thing at a time. The focus might have to switch over from one moment to the next. The stress of life is not in the things but in the switching of things, the constant flow of things, the inability to enjoy the things themselves.

As the bus arrived, I regretted leaving that spot. It had become sacred, silent, and still.

Reflection

- How often do I allow my surroundings to completely ruin my state of mind?
- Do I follow the crowd, or do I remain still, and focus on God's presence?
- Quietly reflect on the following passage: "And behold, the Lord passed by, and a great and strong wind tore the mountains, and broke in pieces the rocks before the Lord, but the Lord was not in the wind; and after the wind an earthquake, but the Lord was not in the earthquake; and after the earthquake a fire, but the Lord was not in the fire; and after the fire a still small voice. And when Eli´jah heard it, he wrapped his face in his mantle" (1 Kings 19:11–13).

CONCLUSION

Death by Komodo Dragon

Or

Don't Be So Busy as to Miss
Life's Greatest Moments

*"See that you do not despise one of these little ones;
for I tell you that in heaven their angels always behold the face of my Father who is in heaven." Matthew 18:10*

It is a funny thing to write a book about the present
moment in a house full of children. How many paragraphs have been interrupted! How many times have I
lost focus when writing about focus! I have developed a
knack for writing about silence with screaming children
around me. The humor of it lightens my spirit and makes
my sentences looser and more agile.

One time when I was writing on stillness, my eight-
year-old, Paul, sat next to me organizing his poker chips
(yes, he plays poker). He started telling me about how

he will get a pocket knife when he turns nine. I stopped typing, pulled my hands away, looked into his eyes, and listened to him for about twenty seconds. I responded with some goofy reply about how he can now live in the woods and hunt his own food. I had been still for him . . . and so I thought I could return to work. The real work, however, had just begun, for Paul was to launch into a brilliant monologue.

> Actually, no, Dad. I can't survive in the woods alone. The knife isn't sharp enough. The animals will get away. And by the way, Komodo dragons can be ten feet long. If a deer gets bit by a Komodo dragon, there is no turning back. It will go through five stages of death: 1) it gets tired; 2) it lays down; 3) it then is nearly dead; 4) its heart starts to stop; 5) then its heart stops and it is finally dead. So I can't survive in the woods with a pocket knife.[6]

Now, if I was typing while he said all that, I would have missed that incredible analysis. My life is enriched for knowing the five stages of death by Komodo dragon.

Parents have a treasure trove of these brilliant insights from their children. But we must stop and listen. We

---

[6]   Somehow, I remembered exactly what he said and typed it up as soon as he left. I have no idea how he got this idea . . . probably from some TV show. But his rendition of the stages of death are brilliant in a kid-like way. They are worth reading again carefully.

must put the cell phone down. We must put e-mail away. We must fold our hands and look them square in the eye. We must take in every second of this great privilege to be a parent.

I have but one life to live. I must live it in the present with silence and with stillness. For one day, I will get tired. I will then lay down. I will be nearly dead. My heart will begin to stop. Then, in God's good time, my heart will stop, and I will be dead.

And by God's grace, I will finally escape the storm and enter into the eternal present moment.

If You Liked This Book . . .

Please give it to someone you think needs it. Pause for a moment and think about your friends and family who are suffering from some form of anxiety or stress or resentment . . . or someone who just lacks peace. Then give them this book and say, "This book really helped me. And I thought of you a few times while I was reading it. It's a quick and easy read. Give it a shot." Then, most importantly, pray for them the next few days.

Bulk Purchases

If you think this book can help lots of people, consider giving it away in bulk. We can offer special discounts for parishes, book clubs, men's or women's conferences, and fraternal organizations. Contact us at 800-437-5876 for pricing.

ABOUT THE AUTHOR

Conor Gallagher graduated with an undergraduate degree in Philosophy from Franciscan University in Steubenville, OH. He then earned both his Masters in Philosophy and Juris Doctorate from the Catholic University of America. He began his professional career as a law clerk to the Honorable Robert J. Conrad, Chief Judge of the Western District of North Carolina. He has been an adjunct Professor of Philosophy and Political Philosophy at Belmont Abbey College, and is currently the Executive Director of the Benedict Leadership Institute at Belmont Abbey College. He is also a proud board member and executive of his eighty-year-old family business, Good Will Publishers, Inc. Gallagher sits on numerous boards, including the Association of Catholic Publishers and Holy Angels, a non-profit residential facility for disabled children and adults.

Gallagher is Publisher of Saint Benedict Press and TAN Books. *Still Amidst the Storm: A Family Man's Search for Peace in an Anxious World* is Gallagher's fourth book. In 2012 he authored *If Aristotle's Kid Had an iPod: Ancient*

Wisdom for Modern Parents, a book for any parent trying to wade through the world of technology and children. In 2014 and 2015 respectively, he authored two other small gift books for parents and children: *First Steps in Your Journey of Faith* and *Parish Life: A Baby Journal from Baptism to First Reconciliation*; and *Pray Always: A Catholic Child's First Prayer Book*.

He and his wife, Ashley, are the proud parents of twelve children: Aiden, Mary, Patrick, Peter, Jude, Paul, Teresa, Imelda, David, Annie, Luke, and Thomas (the twins).

How to Contact Conor Gallagher:

Gallagher is available for interviews and speaking engagements.

Please contact him at PublishersOffice@tanbooks.com.